Navigating through Technology in Modern Education

Authored by

Abdul-Mumin Khalid and Obeng Owusu-Boateng
Department of Mathematics/ICT Education
E. P. College of Education, Bimbilla
Ghana

Navigating through Technology in Modern Education

Authors: Abdul-Mumin Khalid & Obeng Owusu-Boateng

ISBN (Online): 978-981-5238-78-5

ISBN (Print): 978-981-5238-79-2

ISBN (Paperback): 978-981-5238-80-8

© 2024, Bentham Books imprint.

Published by Bentham Science Publishers Pte. Ltd. Singapore. All Rights Reserved.

First published in 2024.

BENTHAM SCIENCE PUBLISHERS LTD.
End User License Agreement (for non-institutional, personal use)

This is an agreement between you and Bentham Science Publishers Ltd. Please read this License Agreement carefully before using the ebook/echapter/ejournal (**"Work"**). Your use of the Work constitutes your agreement to the terms and conditions set forth in this License Agreement. If you do not agree to these terms and conditions then you should not use the Work.

Bentham Science Publishers agrees to grant you a non-exclusive, non-transferable limited license to use the Work subject to and in accordance with the following terms and conditions. This License Agreement is for non-library, personal use only. For a library / institutional / multi user license in respect of the Work, please contact: permission@benthamscience.net.

Usage Rules:

1. All rights reserved: The Work is the subject of copyright and Bentham Science Publishers either owns the Work (and the copyright in it) or is licensed to distribute the Work. You shall not copy, reproduce, modify, remove, delete, augment, add to, publish, transmit, sell, resell, create derivative works from, or in any way exploit the Work or make the Work available for others to do any of the same, in any form or by any means, in whole or in part, in each case without the prior written permission of Bentham Science Publishers, unless stated otherwise in this License Agreement.
2. You may download a copy of the Work on one occasion to one personal computer (including tablet, laptop, desktop, or other such devices). You may make one back-up copy of the Work to avoid losing it.
3. The unauthorised use or distribution of copyrighted or other proprietary content is illegal and could subject you to liability for substantial money damages. You will be liable for any damage resulting from your misuse of the Work or any violation of this License Agreement, including any infringement by you of copyrights or proprietary rights.

Disclaimer:

Bentham Science Publishers does not guarantee that the information in the Work is error-free, or warrant that it will meet your requirements or that access to the Work will be uninterrupted or error-free. The Work is provided "as is" without warranty of any kind, either express or implied or statutory, including, without limitation, implied warranties of merchantability and fitness for a particular purpose. The entire risk as to the results and performance of the Work is assumed by you. No responsibility is assumed by Bentham Science Publishers, its staff, editors and/or authors for any injury and/or damage to persons or property as a matter of products liability, negligence or otherwise, or from any use or operation of any methods, products instruction, advertisements or ideas contained in the Work.

Limitation of Liability:

In no event will Bentham Science Publishers, its staff, editors and/or authors, be liable for any damages, including, without limitation, special, incidental and/or consequential damages and/or damages for lost data and/or profits arising out of (whether directly or indirectly) the use or inability to use the Work. The entire liability of Bentham Science Publishers shall be limited to the amount actually paid by you for the Work.

General:

1. Any dispute or claim arising out of or in connection with this License Agreement or the Work (including non-contractual disputes or claims) will be governed by and construed in accordance with the laws of Singapore. Each party agrees that the courts of the state of Singapore shall have exclusive jurisdiction to settle any dispute or claim arising out of or in connection with this License Agreement or the Work (including non-contractual disputes or claims).
2. Your rights under this License Agreement will automatically terminate without notice and without the

need for a court order if at any point you breach any terms of this License Agreement. In no event will any delay or failure by Bentham Science Publishers in enforcing your compliance with this License Agreement constitute a waiver of any of its rights.
3. You acknowledge that you have read this License Agreement, and agree to be bound by its terms and conditions. To the extent that any other terms and conditions presented on any website of Bentham Science Publishers conflict with, or are inconsistent with, the terms and conditions set out in this License Agreement, you acknowledge that the terms and conditions set out in this License Agreement shall prevail.

Bentham Science Publishers Pte. Ltd.
80 Robinson Road #02-00
Singapore 068898
Singapore
Email: subscriptions@benthamscience.net

CONTENTS

PREFACE i

CHAPTER 1 INTRODUCTION TO DIGITAL TRANSFORMATION IN THE EDUCATION SECTOR 1
- **1. INTRODUCTION** 1
- **2. LITERATURE** 2
  - 2.1. Digital Transformation 2
    - 2.1.2. DT in Educational Sector 3
    - 2.1.3. Types of Technologies Use in the Educational Sector 3
    - 2.1.4. Robot Educator 3
    - 2.1.5. VR/AR 4
    - 2.1.6. Big Data 4
    - 2.1.7. Classroom Devices 5
    - 2.1.8. Mobile Devices 5
    - 2.1.9. Robotic 3D Printing 5
    - 2.1.10. A High-Tech Classroom 5
    - 2.1.11. Gamification 6
    - 2.1.12. IoT 6
    - 2.1.13. Customized Learning 7
    - 2.1.14. Learning Management System 7
    - 2.1.15 Artificial Intelligence 8
    - 2.1.16. Scope of DT in Education 8
    - 2.1.17. Technology 10
    - 2.1.18. Strategies for IT, IS 10
- **3. IMPLICATIONS** 11
  - 3.1. The Future of Technology in the Education Sector 13
  - **CONCLUSION** 13
  - **REFERENCES** 13

CHAPTER 2 DIGITAL TRANSFORMATION IN THE EDUCATION SECTOR: BENEFITS AND CHALLENGES 16
- **1. INTRODUCTION** 16
- **2. LITERATURE** 17
  - 2.1. Benefits of Technology in the Education Sector 17
    - 2.1.1. Challenges of DT in the Education Sector 29
- **3. DISCUSSION** 41
- **4. IMPLICATIONS** 42
- **CONCLUSION** 43
- **REFERENCES** 44

CHAPTER 3 FACTORS FOR ADOPTING TECHNOLOGY IN THE EDUCATION SECTOR 46
- **1. INTRODUCTION** 46
  - 1.1. Contributions of the Chapters 48
- **2. LITERATURE** 48
  - 2.1. Digital Transformation 48
  - 2.2. Digital Transformation in Education 48
  - 2.3. Factors 49
  - 2.4. The Educator, Professor, or Lecturer 50
  - 2.5. Factors in Context 50
  - 2.6. Governmental Actions 51
  - 2.7. University Factors 51

    2.8. Organizational Culture and Leadership ... 51
    2.9. Skills in Information and Communication Technology ... 52
  3. OBTAINABILITY OF RESOURCES ... 52
    3.1. Involved Parties, Value, and Developments ... 52
    3.2. Advances in Technology ... 53
    3.3. Superiority of Information ... 53
    3.4. Data Science and Business Intelligence ... 54
    3.5. Compatibility ... 54
  4. IMPLICATIONS ... 54
  CONCLUSION ... 55
  RECOMMENDATIONS ... 55
  REFERENCES ... 56

CHAPTER 4 THE ADOPTION OF E-LEARNING IN THE EDUCATION SECTOR ... 59
  1. INTRODUCTION ... 59
    1.1. Contribution ... 60
  2. LITERATURE ... 61
    2.1. E-Learning ... 61
    2.2 Factors for Adopting E-Learning ... 62
      2.2.1. Subjective Norm ... 62
      2.2.2. Culture ... 62
      2.2.3. The Interaction of Systems ... 62
      2.2.4. Unique to Each Educational Institution ... 63
      2.2.5. Convenience ... 64
      2.2.6. Self-Efficacy ... 64
      2.2.7. Accessibility ... 64
      2.2.8. Personal/Individual Factors ... 64
      2.2.9. Technical Factors ... 65
      2.2.10. Flexibility ... 65
      2.2.11. Environmental Factors ... 66
      2.2.12. Technology Factors ... 66
      2.2.13. Smart-Device Use ... 68
  3. DISCUSSION ... 68
  4. IMPLICATIONS ... 69
  CONCLUSION ... 70
  RECOMMENDATIONS ... 71
  REFERENCES ... 71

CHAPTER 5 THE ADOPTION OF ARTIFICIAL INTELLIGENCE IN THE EDUCATION SECTOR ... 75
  1. INTRODUCTION ... 75
  2. LITERATURE ... 76
    2.1. Artificial Intelligence (AI) ... 76
    2.2. Adoption of AI in the Education Sector ... 77
    2.3. Benefits of AI Adoption in the Education Sector ... 78
    2.4. Future of Artificial Intelligence in the Educational Sector ... 83
  3. IMPLICATIONS ... 84
  CONCLUSION ... 84
  REFERENCES ... 85

CHAPTER 6 THE ADOPTION OF BIG DATA IN THE EDUCATION SECTOR ... 87
  1. INTRODUCTION ... 87

1.1. Contributions	89
2. LITERATURE	90
2.1. Big Data (BD)	90
2.2. Adoption of Big Data in the Education Sector	91
2.3. Factors for Adopting BD in the Education Sector	92
2.4. Perceived Usefulness	92
2.5. Perceived Ease of Use (PEOU)	93
2.6. Perceived Credibility (PC)	99
2.7. Environmental Factors	100
2.8. Organizational Factors	101
3. BENEFITS OF BIG DATA IN THE EDUCATION SECTOR	103
4. THE FUTURE OF BIG DATA IN EDUCATION	106
5. IMPLICATIONS	106
CONCLUSION	108
REFERENCES	109
CHAPTER 7 THE ADOPTION OF THE INTERNET OF THINGS (IOT) IN THE EDUCATION SECTOR	113
1. INTRODUCTION	113
2. LITERATURE	114
2.1. Internet of Things (IoT)	114
2.2. Adoption of Internet of Things in the Education Sector	115
2.3. Benefits of IoTs in the Education Sector	116
3. DISADVANTAGES OF IOTS IN EDUCATION	124
4. IMPLICATIONS	128
CONCLUSION	129
REFERENCES	130
SUBJECT INDEX	132

PREFACE

The evolution of technological advances has transitioned from individual initiatives to interconnected networks of tools and programs that facilitate global connectivity and contribute to the resolution of both personal and global issues. The utilization of digital innovation has exhibited capabilities to supplement, enhance, and revolutionize the field of education. The significance of digitization in the education industry cannot be overstated. The utilization of technology in education provides enhanced opportunities for both students and teachers, facilitates a more welcoming and practical learning environment for individuals with disabilities, and contributes to the improvement of engagement among students. Digital transformation in education has a profound effect on enhancing the learning experience for students, teachers, and other stakeholders engaged in the educational process. These modifications prioritize enhancing student involvement and ease of use by incorporating interactive elements and allowing for personalized learning experiences. Consequently, online education has become more affordable, extensive, and accessible. The book covers a wide range of topics:

Introduction to Digital Transformation in the Education Sector

Digital Transformation in the Education Sector: Benefits and Challenges

Factors for Adopting Technology in the Education Sector

Adoption of E-Learning in the Education Sector

The Adoption of Artificial Intelligence in the Education sector

The Adoption of Big Data in the Education Sector

The Adoption of the Internet of Things in the Education Sector

CHAPTER 1

Introduction to Digital Transformation in the Education Sector

Abstract: The social behaviors of humans have been profoundly impacted by recent developments in hardware and software technologies, from education to health, transport, manufacturing and trade. By transferring physical education into digital formats, COVID-19's effects on education have significantly accelerated digital evolution in Ghana and around the world. Education received a lot of attention during the Industrial Revolution of the twenty-first century. However, a few of the difficulties in getting data from the source to the end consumers are the expense of the infrastructure, problems with network connectivity, and digital platforms. Another criterion for assessing the progress of digitization and its effects on developing and developed nations is the economic variety of the populace. Personalized learning, academic advising, data collecting, management, and other areas are all heavily reliant on digital transformation, which highlights a trend.

Keywords: Digital Transformation, Education, Internet, Technology, University.

1. INTRODUCTION

From the publishing industry to the music business, the Internet has had a profound effect on the dissemination of information. The field of education is also undergoing a period of transformation. These days, "digital transformation" is a buzzword on every teacher's lips. The COVID-19 pandemic has prompted a shift in how technological advances are used in educational settings (Al-Shakarchi, 2022). Stakeholders in the education system include students, faculty, parents/guardians, and government/regulatory agencies. The necessity for effective operation, cost management, and performance in terms of set goals is, however, universal across all organizational contexts (Gartner, 2023). To better serve both their students and teachers, higher education institutions are undergoing a digital transition. To fully realize the benefits of the digital age and a digital revolution necessitates rethinking traditional methods of instruction and administration. However, because of advances in technology and new ways of thinking, it is now possible to convert lecture materials into digital form and make them widely available online. Not only does this necessitate cutting-edge tools,

Abdul-Mumin Khalid & Obeng Owusu-Boateng
All rights reserved-© 2024 Bentham Science Publishers

but also cutting-edge practices. Not just technical expertise but also command of management is an extremely scarce commodity in the field of education. Prospective leaders in today's organizations need to be able to sort through a plethora of digital projects, accelerate innovative cycles, and restructure their organizations to better accommodate novel methods. Students in the modern era need access to a wealth of digital materials. Prospective students are continuously on the lookout for innovative educational possibilities that go beyond the standard lecture format. To provide high-quality education, educational institutions must innovate and adapt to meet the changing demands of today's students. One of the hallmarks of our day is the widespread adoption of digital technologies. It appears that developing nations are falling behind in these areas as the fourth industrial revolution (Industry 4.0) is examined through digitization and things such as the internet, big data, coding, and smart manufacturing (Parlak, 2017). Industry 4.0, as defined by Bates (2015), places an emphasis on education that is relevant to the requirements of an economic order and a market transformed by digital technology. Our educational system is not in sync with these ideas; today's students are still being taught in classrooms that appear little different from those of decades past, and the demands of modern education are being ignored, at least in part. Therefore, all students in postsecondary education must have the knowledge and skills necessary to make effective use of information and communication technologies (ICT) and digital learning technology in the classroom. The purpose of this chapter is to serve as a guide for further research on the correlation between students' ICT engagement and their digital learning. The implementation and utilization of instructional technologies have proven challenging in developing countries and have not always resulted in proportional advances in student learning outcomes. The chapter moves in this approach by thinking about how online settings will change the nature, breadth, and method of schooling.

2. LITERATURE

2.1. Digital Transformation

The term "digital transformation" encompasses a wide range of concepts, from IT upgrades (such as cloud computing) to process improvements and even the creation of entirely novel digital business models. Many government agencies use this word to describe relatively small projects like moving services online or updating older systems (Gartner, 2023) because of budgetary constraints. A digital revolution, as defined by Norton *et al.* (2020), is a shift in the way labor is organized due to the introduction of new digital technology and business strategies. It is more than just dropping in a new piece of software; it requires harmony among digital tools, people, and structures. Digital transformation, as defined by Mahlow and Hediger (2019), involves the strategic and in-depth development of new competencies and models *via* digital technology.

2.1.2. DT in Educational Sector

Incorporating technology into the classroom has been shown to greatly improve students' engagement with course material. For instance, since many students learn best by seeing rather than hearing, schools can benefit from having projection screens connected to computers so students can glance at their notes instead of just sitting and listening to the teacher. The class set of courses is standardized using different technologies (Mustapha, 2018). To help students keep learning even when they are not in class, these technologies consolidate a variety of learning resources into a single location, such as study questions, examinations, and exercises. It is encouraging that technology may play a wide variety of roles in the classroom, from supplementing more traditional methods to replacing them entirely. Given the foregoing, it is clear that many learners have benefited from the incorporation of technology into the classroom. Mustapha (2018) and Akinsola and Animashun (2007) are right to draw attention to the significance of technology in the classroom.

2.1.3. Types of Technologies Use in the Educational Sector

As has been seen above, the digital revolution is not a novel idea or process in education; rather, it is a global phenomenon that has already shown promising results in some places (World Economic Forum, 2016). In this section, we will look at six patterns that help define what the digital revolution means in the real world (Aleksandrov et al., 2018): 1) Augmented, Virtual, and Mixed Reality (AR, VR, and MR), (2) Tools for the Classroom, (3) Remodeled Classrooms, () Machine learning/AI, (5) Customized Instruction, and (6) The Use of Games. Looking at successful implementations of digital advances in education strengthens professional bonds and gives teachers more agency. Teachers at all levels are learning the benefits of using technology in the educational setting.

2.1.4. Robot Educator

Making robots that can teach is a multi-faceted endeavor. Learning robots are a clear example of the fruition of interdisciplinary research and development to aid in the classroom. It has the potential to pique students' attention, encourage their creative potential, and make better use of information technology to expand their horizons and expand their access to information. Learning robots are smart teaching tools that can serve as a potent adjunct to teachers in a variety of classroom settings. By interacting with a computer, students can improve their capacity to study independently and actively seek solutions to problems. The emotions of the students are read by learning robots. As a result of increased interaction with students, educators will have a better idea of how to tailor their instruction to each student's unique strengths and weaknesses. This will allow for a more personalized learning experience for everyone.

2.1.5. VR/AR

The field of augmented and virtual reality is very young, and it will be some time before these technologies have a significant impact on classroom instruction. Transformative technologies like augmented, virtual, and mixed reality enhance teaching by providing students with more realistic and interesting environments in which to learn. The world beyond the classroom can be brought in through the use of virtual reality technology. Currently, they are useful in the classroom since they let pupils to better imagine and grasp abstract ideas and locations. Students can now use augmented reality in the classroom or outside of it to see visual images of scientific subjects. However, using virtual reality, kids may experience informative field trips without leaving the classroom. When combined, the two technologies are revolutionizing classroom practices and providing students with more engaging educational opportunities. In a nutshell, it makes learning enjoyable and engaging (Clarifi Education PBC., 2023) for them. The interactive nature of AR/VR education allows for a more engaging and personal learning experience. Students benefit from this and remain interested. Learn anything, anywhere, at any time with augmented reality and virtual reality apps. This is the most practical alternative to traditional media like books, posters, large models, *etc.*

2.1.6. Big Data

Big Data is shorthand for "huge amounts of data", which can be defined as data sets that contain information on humans, their surroundings, and their relationships with each other. In a similar vein, "Educational Big Data" refers to the technology resources utilized by educators to amass meaningful data rapidly and cheaply. Big Data are distinguished by their 5 Vs (li & Jiang, 2021): volume, because of the vast amounts of data they can store; velocity, because of the ease with which they can be analyzed; variety, because they are fed data from a wide range of sources; veracity, because of the quality of the data; and value, because of the substantial benefit they provide. Similarly, a bibliometric analysis of recent research reveals emerging tendencies in Big Data as they pertain to e-learning, online learning, student engagement, the influence of psychological aspects, and the role of social media. Big data may be used to collect large amounts of valuable data quickly, cheaply, and with high quality by making use of their veracity, variety, value, velocity, and volume in the classroom. This is an important lesson for educators.

2.1.7. Classroom Devices

To move away from the standard of having students follow the BYOD (Bring Your Own Device) policy, the field of educational technology has purchased a set of gadgets for use in classrooms. Also, they might avoid going to libraries or universities just to use a computer. Laptops, tablets, and iPads are standard issues in most classrooms today. Due to the ever-present nature of the internet, they also need to be cognizant of the importance of cyber security.

2.1.8. Mobile Devices

Students can use their mobile phones or smartphones with preloaded apps for a variety of pedagogical objectives. They have easy access to resources like Google and YouTube, as well as social networking sites. They have access to a plethora of online educational resources, such as webinars, discussion boards, and virtual classrooms. The use of mobile devices for testing is also viewed as a sort of educational technology (EdTech) and digital transformation. Medical, biological, engineering, mathematical, scientific, technological, *etc.*, can all be taught with the use of digital transformation (Alrofouh et al., 2019). The use of a smartphone is another option for mobile learning. Appropriate use of a smartphone has been shown to improve academic outcomes (Amez & Baert, 2020). There is a correlation between pedagogical strategy and student achievement (Andrey & Martin, 2013). Laptops and mobile phones (smartphones) are just two examples of mobile technologies that can be used as learning tools. The potential for these gadgets to enhance the educational experience is enormous. A recent meta-analysis and study synthesis of 110 experimental journal publications (Sung et al., 2016) found that mobile devices are useful learning tools both inside and outside the classroom.

2.1.9. Robotic 3D Printing

It is a cutting-edge tool for the classroom that lets pupils model everything from artworks to scientific instruments in three dimensions. Students' originality in conceiving school projects can benefit from this.

2.1.10. A High-Tech Classroom

Due to technological advancements, educational institutions have become more up-to-date and functional. Smart classrooms, which incorporate networked computers, projectors, tablets, and software, emerged as a result. As a result, classroom instruction is assisted and students' attention is drawn to the material being taught. To enhance the educational process, "Smart Classes" implement technological solutions. Using a variety of audio and visual aids enhances and enriches the learning process (Polych, 2023) for the student. Specialized software is designed and fine-tuned to satisfy the needs of a certain category, as opposed to being a one-size-fits-all solution. The digital infrastructure enhances both instructor-student and student-student communication due to its isolation and organization of data streams. One such feature is the "raise hand" option included in many video conferencing programs. The advantages of using them could also be discussed in Smart Classes. Students will have more original ideas when they get home (Polych, 2023) because of this. Once a standard in education, lectures are now rarely used in today's schools. Students can gain a lot from engaging in collaborative learning activities. Projectors and computers facilitate the sharing of data. Interactive touch displays have the potential to engross students.

2.1.11. Gamification

Learners can earn electronic badges or awards for reaching academic milestones with the help of this technology. It is a great way to keep score and see how your team stacks up against others. Clarifi Education PBC. (2023) reports that students' interest in and motivation for schoolwork has increased as a result of gamification. The goal of gamifying the learning process is to appeal to students' intrinsic motivations to increase their level of participation and proficiency. People who take part in this method of skill development have preferences for drama, tradition, and fun. The player's genuine character emerges under pressure or in a heightened state of curiosity in a gamified system. Instead of relying on grades and degrees, this approach to hiring experts could be a good one. Thanks to its open nature, gamification reveals each student's potential, thinking style, and logical prowess. A trained educator can then use this information to correctly identify the child's interests and guide his or her growth accordingly.

2.1.12. IoT

IoT is favored by today's educational institutions, which employ a wide range of approaches, from AR to cloud computing, to better educate their students. Internet of Things (IoT) technology integration is an example of a pervasive digital revolution in education, leading to smarter and more networked physical environments than ever before. The Internet of Things (IoT) has several potential applications in the classroom, including the introduction of technologies like smart boards, digital signage, and voice command systems (Polych, 2023) that are already in use. However, thanks to advancements in IoT, schools can now deploy smart security cameras, automate student attendance tracking, and keep parents updated on when their children are ready to be picked up from school.

2.1.13. Customized Learning

In a significant way, educational technology has allowed for more individualized instruction. Students can receive individualized instruction in any setting, be it a traditional schoolroom, a student's own home, or an online forum. It allows them to tailor their education to their individual goals and strengths. More student agencies emerged as a result of blended learning. They need to have one-on-one time with educators and use a discovery approach to education (Clarifi Education PBC., 2023) to succeed.

2.1.14. Learning Management System

Learning management systems (LMS) are among the most widely adopted examples of digital transformation in the classroom. These systems facilitate the creation and management of training courses, communication between instructors and students, the planning and organization of all educational processes, and the tracking of data regarding the effectiveness of instructional materials and the growth of individual students. The core of any educational LMS should be online courses. With this capability, virtual classroom instruction should be feasible. Any scholastic resource can be downloaded, together with tests, exam forms, student results, *etc.* In fact, according to research (Polych, 2023), this function should encompass all the steps involved in efficient learning. Common misconception: LMSs are exclusively used to manage online courses. However, it is not limited to just online or hybrid courses. This is made possible through numerous channels of information exchange, such as webcasts, message boards, live chats, and electronic newsletters. In-person, online, one-on-one, or group instruction can all be coordinated with the aid of a learning management system. Schools can use this function to make changes to existing training courses or entirely remove them. Thanks to this function, both educators and students will have an easier time keeping track of what they need to study. Students and instructors can maintain constant communication through virtual meetings. Using the live chat feature, any questions the students may have can be answered quickly. Using internet video chats, educators and students can hold virtual classes whenever and wherever works best for them (Polych, 2023). You can use this function to design and modify instructional materials, including multimedia files like images, animations and videos. You may control not only which users have access to which courses but also which courses they can download. Web-based learning management systems (LMS) and virtual learning environments (VLE) combine teaching and learning resources with administrative features (Ifenthaler, 2012).

They can be used to coordinate all aspects of a course, including instruction, assessment, and supplemental instruction. They make it easy to store and organize various forms of media (lectures, readings, videos, *etc.*) so that students can access them whenever they like. Chat rooms are available for both student and teacher interaction. They contain features that enable user and class management (such as a syllabus, student activity tracking, and office hour scheduling) (Ifenthaler, 2021).

2.1.15 Artificial Intelligence

Finally, one of the greatest advantages of technology for students is the usage of artificial intelligence. Education is made available to students around the clock, routine tasks are automated, and people from all over the world have access to information that can assist them in filling in knowledge gaps (Polych, 2023) because of this innovation. To put it another way, AI has expanded the possibilities of individualized education and is helping students find solutions to problems more quickly.

2.1.16. Scope of DT in Education

Broad in scope, digital transitions are common. A company's digital transformation plan is a road map that helps it manage the changes that occur as a result of adopting digital technologies and continues to serve the company after the transition is complete. Changes in a company's business model, such as new goods, reorganized departments, or automated procedures, are the focus of digital transformation. The increasing popularity of online media consumption is one indicator of these shifts, as it has caused entire industries (the music business, for instance) to rethink their approaches to doing business. The application of cutting-edge digital tools (such as social media, handheld devices, data mining, or embedded devices) leads to substantial business gains (like better serving customers, cutting costs, or developing innovative strategies). In 2018, Liere-Netheler and co-authors defined the term "digital transformation" as the process by which a company replaces or complements its physical offerings with digital ones, including the company's sales and communication routes and the goods and services it provides. In addition, data-driven insights and the introduction of electronic company structures that permit new ways of generating value are catalysts for the operational and broader business activities that constitute digital transformation.

- **Process**

A departure from conventional methods of production and the distribution of value to customers is what digitization entails. The use of digital media to improve upon or supplant analog goods and services is included, along with the corresponding operational processes involved in doing so (Sandkuhl & Lehmann, 2017). In the procedural dimensions, new and IT-operable stages are developed to optimize existing procedures and facilitate the seamless incorporation of novel features into existing ones (Ebert & Duarte, 2018). According to Balyer and Oz (2018), modern, student-centered assessment and evaluation approaches should replace the outmoded, group-focused ones now used in education. According to Sandkuhl and Lehmann (2017), all of the steps in the college application process (including admission, program and course registration, course examination, the establishment of programs, quality assurance, *etc.*) contribute to the production of value for the student. Support for mobile workers and managing information are essential features of an integrated campus management system.

- **People**

Organizations with advanced technological capabilities are more likely to undergo a digital transformation, which will have far-reaching effects on the company as a whole, including its departments, positions, duties, and structure (Mahmood et al., 2019). Not only business but also academia has entered the "4.0" era. The difficulty is in training students and faculty for the rapid technological developments, new decentralized governance paradigms, expanding importance of AI, and other continuing changes (Richert Anja et al., 2016). Participants should help colleges and universities undergo a digital transformation by providing them with access to educational materials and resources that are suitable for modern technology, regardless of location or time of day. Experts in the field of higher education, including both directors and program experts, are prepared for and equipped to handle this transition in addition to bringing about beneficial shifts for the school's administration, faculty, and students. To be ready for the digital transformation, it must complete the essential initial and ongoing training (Balyer & Oz, 2018).

- **Data**

The keeping of all of the information belonging to an organization, the comprehension of the data gathered and obtainable for evaluation, the classification of data assets, the evaluation of data quality, and the pursuit of opportunities to integrate data resources all present difficulties for organizations undergoing a digital shift. Information presents both advantages and disadvantages. According to Heaven and Power (2018), useless data is of no value. A thorough analysis of information provides new ways of gaining insight into educational practices, as emphasized by Digitalisierung (2016) in their discussion of the connection between technology progress and recent trends in educational institutions. The college system is made more open and comparable by the methodical gathering and evaluation of the information that has been gathered. Improving teaching quality and learning environments requires an in-depth understanding of the mechanisms involved in both. According to Maltese (2018), colleges now face different issues as a result of the digital revolution. In particular, the capacity to furnish users with comprehensive, current, and reliable data across a variety of channels of interaction and online resources. Institutions require it.

2.1.17. Technology

Companies' transition into digital environments is enabled by digital technologies. Companies can seize new opportunities made possible by technological advances. Business models, operational procedures, and customer experiences are just a few areas that could be affected by these prospects. As a result, the positive effects of this change can be seen throughout the company (Morakanyane et al., 2017). The use of technological advances in education is now widespread. University technology has progressed to the point where it can help shape classrooms and other study spaces around the needs of individual students (Reigeluth, 2014). The digital transformation process calls for the implementation of distance learning apps and the integration of ICT into traditional classroom settings. These digital tools for implementing digital transformation are crucial to education. For the sake of students' private data, it can be released either en masse by a coordinating body or wholly independently. Participation in the educational setting should be facilitated through the use of technology for communication and information use (Balyer & Oz, 2018). To improve student agency and satisfaction, technology must live up to or surpass students' high expectations (Munro, 2018).

2.1.18. Strategies for IT, IS

The shift to digital technology does not follow a single principle. Strategies for IT, IS, handling change, and marketing are all part of this. Such tactics must be in sync with one another for the shift to go smoothly (Mahmood et al., 2019). Industry and business strategies for digital transformation should have four key components, as recommended by Matt (2015): technology saturation, value-creation-model shifts, structure-shifting, and money-related concerns. Organization-wide digitization is a challenging task. Implementing technological change plans requires a methodical approach. According to Hess *et al.* (2016), management needs to modify the value generation dimensions to meet the needs of their business models.

- **Product/Service**

If you have an educational service or product, According to Sandkuhl and Lehmann (2017), schools should prioritize the development of new educational materials and the digitization of current ones, allowing students from all over the world to participate in nationally and internationally recognized academic programs and integrating online and distance learning into conventional teaching methods. In most cases, this means adopting a digital strategy for delivering course materials and facilitating student-teacher and student-student communication and cooperation (Balyer & Oz, 2018).

- **Digital Practices**

In colleges and universities, "digital practices" refer to how both faculty and students (in both academic and extracurricular roles) utilize and adjust to digital technologies during their daily work and study. For example, while teaching a course online or in a hybrid format, a professor may rethink some of the course's fundamentals, such as its structure or its assessment methods. It may also involve how students structure the time they spend studying or network with teachers and classmates to facilitate their education. Learning resources and support, such as guidance on future endeavors, are provided to pupils. The government's use of digitalization in system management is also covered, such as in performance evaluation and resource allocation. This initiative takes a broad view of the use of digital tools in higher education. So, we may say that "online learning" is the same as "digitally-enhanced teaching and learning". Both of these concepts are synonymous with what is known as "e-learning" by the European Association for Quality Assurance in Education (ENQA). Massive open online courses (MOOCs), open educational resources (OER), and hybrid/blended learning (designed to combine online and in-person teaching in any combination) are all included in ENQA's definition of e-learning (Huertas et al., 2018).

3. IMPLICATIONS

Future education policy should be geared toward this digital transition in schooling. It is important to build long-term strategies for carrying out technological education policies. The contexts and methods through which digital technologies are introduced into higher education affect the relationship between digital preparedness, behaviors, and outcomes. Several factors contribute to the uniqueness of each higher education environment, such as the level and field of study offered, the orientation and selectivity of the institution, and the demographic and academic profile of the student body. Whether or not digital technologies are used for all teaching and learning activities (e.g., lectures, small group classes, self-directed learning, and assessment) is one example of how digital technologies are implemented. How well institutions and their staff have prepared for the implementation of digitally enhanced courses and programs is also a factor. During the coronavirus (COVID-19) pandemic, the sudden transition to online learning made this approach impossible. In this light, it has become clear that the service, management, learning environments, and instructional programs given by educational institutions must also transform in tandem with digitization to meet the needs of individuals. One may argue that digital transformation is both a vision and a strategy in addition to being technology-based. Top-level decision-makers must keep this long-term goal in mind as they craft education policy and then put it into action, beginning with the design and construction of necessary physical facilities. It is the correct thing to do if we want the stakeholders in our educational system to have a say in shaping our policies and our vision. It is important to specify in advance what is anticipated from future generations and the school, and how to train persons, in addition to the policies to be determined in this context. Society must be prepared for the digital transformation process that will take place in schools. Managers in the education industry should be aware of the need to acquire digital competence, which can be defined as the ability to grasp digital tools for pedagogical purposes and to use those tools effectively. Because of this, they may more easily incorporate technology into their teaching without sacrificing quality. Training in these digital skills extends far beyond familiarity with specific platforms or familiarity with specific digital tools and their networks; rather, it permeates all aspects of students' lives, fostering the development of a digital culture and facilitating the production of content that is both original and adaptable, as well as up-to-date at the same rate that new digital resources are introduced into the classroom. This will enable them to adopt an objective stance to critically evaluate their application, pinpoint restrictions, and provide solutions to problems. If shareholders are on board with the idea of providing equipment, it becomes much simpler for businesses to offer ongoing maintenance and repair services, as well as back up municipal governments. Students, instructors, and administrators will all benefit from the good cultural shift brought on by the fact that other public institutions and organizations serve as role models for digital transformation culture and help institutions offering education services. Pre-service and in-service training is essential for administrators, instructors, and students to be fully prepared for the digital transition. Furthermore, the next generation of educators must be trained as individuals with this perspective during their time at university. Success has also been attained in appointing managers, recognizing pupils admitted to schools of education, and paying attention to the presence of people with this vision in classrooms.

3.1. The Future of Technology in the Education Sector

Technology and digitalization have had a profound impact on educational systems around the world. However, this raises a significant query. Is modern learning facilitated by digital means? Here are a few arguments for why the use of technology in classrooms is here to stay. The use of eLearning platforms and other forms of EdTech has benefited students by teaching them fundamental technical skills that will be useful in their future careers. The majority of learners find studying to be tedious. Additionally, preschoolers with a shorter attention span struggle to maintain concentration on their schoolwork. They improved their grades and enthusiasm in school thanks to innovative study aids like games and virtual worlds. Students' hunger for knowledge was sated when they discovered a treasure trove of unbounded data regarding topics of interest to them. They can satisfy their insatiable curiosity about any topic by reading reliable accounts of it. Teachers and learners can work together more effectively because of technological advancements in the classroom, facilitating group work on a single assignment among students in numerous places. It is a similar way that educators can engage with pupils and lend assistance. Teachers now have access to more resources, which has improved their ability to teach and guide learners. Learners are more likely to retain information presented in an auditory or visual format. In addition, educators can acquire new skills and update their expertise to better serve their students (Clarifi Education PBC., 2023) using such resources.

CONCLUSION

There are now more ways than ever to provide engaging and fruitful education thanks to the advent of digitalization. The benefits of digital education can be realized both in and out of the classroom through the creation of adaptive, interactive, and student-centered learning spaces. A thorough strategy must be applied to the change if the organization is to reap the benefits of the transformation in full. Based on the analysis, the following are within the purview of DT's scope: 1) Strategy, 2) Process, 3) Product/Service, 4) People, 5) Data, and 6) Technology.

REFERENCES

Aleksandrov, A.A., Kapyrin, P.A., Meshkov, N. A., Popovich, A.E., Proletarsky, A.V. (2018). Gamification in the advanced higher professional education: Fundamentals of theory and experience of use. *Int. J. Civil Eng. Techn., 9*(11), 1800-1808.

Al-Shakarchi, M. (2022). Digital Transformation in Education: The Complete Guide. Available from: https://www.d2l.com/en-eu/blog/digital-transformation-in-education-complete-guide/

Alrofouh, A.M., Lakulu, M.M., Almaiah, M.A. (2019). A Systematic Review of Mobile-Based Assessment Acceptance Studies From 2009 To 2019. *J. Theor. Appl. Inf. Technol., 97*(20), 2530-2553.

Amez, S., Baert, S. (2020). Smartphone use and academic performance: A literature review. *Int. J. Educ.*

Res., *103*(February), 101618.
[http://dx.doi.org/10.1016/j.ijer.2020.101618]

Andrey, Z., Martin, C.P.L. (2014). Which teaching practices improve student performance on high-stakes exams? Evidence from russia basic research program. *In Basic Research Program Working Paper Series: Education., 36*(May), 13-21.

Akinsola, M., Animashun, I. (2007). The effect of simulation-games environment on student achievement in and attitudes to mathematics in secondary schools. *Turk. Online J. Educ. Technol., 6*(3), 113-119.

Bates, T. (2015). Teaching in a digital age: Guidelines for designing teaching and learning for a digital age. Available from: https://opentextbc.ca/teachinginadigitalage/

Balyer, A., Oz, O. (2018). Academicians' views on digital transformation in education. *Int. Online J. Educ. Teach., 5*(4), 809-830. [IOJET].

Digitalisierung, H. (2016). 20 Theses on Digital Teaching and Learning in Higher Education.

Gartner, (2023). Digital Transformation. Available from: https://www.gartner.com/en/information-technology/glossary/digital-transformation

Huertas, E. (2018). *Considerations for Quality Assurance of E-learning Provision.* (pp. 1-22). Brussels: European Association for Quality Assurance in Higher Education.https://www.enqa.eu/wp-content/uploads/Considerations-for-QA-of-e-learning-provision.pdf

Heavin, C., Power, D.J. (2018). Challenges for digital transformation – towards a conceptual decision support guide for managers. *J. Decis. Syst., 27*(S1), 38-45.
[http://dx.doi.org/10.1080/12460125.2018.1468697]

Hess, T., Matt, C., Benlian, A., Wiesböck, F. (2016). Options for formulating a digital transformation strategy. *MIS Q. Exec., 15*(2), 103-119.

Ifenthaler, D. (2021). Paper prepared for the European Commission-Hungary-OECD project "Supporting the Digital Transformation of Hungarian Higher Education". *Student-centred Perspective in the Digitalisation of Higher Education*

Ifenthaler, D. (2012). Learning Management System.*Encyclopedia of the Sciences of Learning..* Boston: Springer.
[http://dx.doi.org/10.1007/978-1-4419-1428-6_187]

Li, J., Jiang, Y. (2021). The Research Trend of Big Data in Education and the Impact of Teacher Psychology on Educational Development During COVID-19: A Systematic Review and Future Perspective. *Front. Psychol., 12*, 753388.
[http://dx.doi.org/10.3389/fpsyg.2021.753388] [PMID: 34777150]

Mahmood, F., Khan, A.Z., Khan, M.B. (2019). Digital organizational transformation issues, challenges and impact: A systematic literature review of a decade. *Abasyn J. Social Sci., 12*(2), 231-249.
[http://dx.doi.org/10.34091/AJSS.12.2.03]

Morakanyane, R., Grace, A., O'Reilly, P. (2017). Conceptualizing digital transformation in business organizations: A systematic review of literature. 30th Bled EConference: Digital Transformation - From Connecting Things to Transforming Our Lives. *BLED, 2017*, 427-443.
[http://dx.doi.org/10.18690/978-961-286-043-1.30]

Munro, M. (2018). The complicity of digital technologies in the marketisation of UK higher education: exploring the implications of a critical discourse analysis of thirteen national digital teaching and learning strategies. *Int. J. Educ. Technol. High. Educ., 15*(1), 11.
[http://dx.doi.org/10.1186/s41239-018-0093-2]

Mahlow, C., Hediger, A. (2019). Digital Transformation in Higher Education-Buzzword or Opportunity? *eLearn Magazine, 2019*(5), 13.

Mustapha, A. (2018). The importance of Technology in Teaching and learning.*Teaching with Technology: Perspectives, Challenges and Future Challenges..* New York: Nova Science Publishers.

Mustapha, A. (2016). Effects of simulation on the achievement, retention and skill performance of motor vehicle mechanic in Niger State technical colleges [unpublished med thesis]. *Minna: National Open University of Nigeria.*

Norton, A., Shroff, S., Edwards, N. (2020). *Digital Transformation: An Enterprise Architecture Perspective..* UK: Publish Nation Limited.

OECD. (2019). *Going Digital: Shaping Policies, Improving Lives..* Paris: OECD Publishing.

Parlak, B. (2017). Dijital çağda eğitim: Olanaklar ve uygulamalar üzerine bir analiz [Education in Digital Age: An analysis on opportunities and practices], Süleyman Demirel University. *J. Faculty Economics Administrative Sci., 22*(15), 1741-1759.

Polych, V. (2023). Digital Transformation in Education: Trends, Problems, and Best Practice [Update]. *Northell.* Available from: https://northell.design/blog/digital-transformation-in-education

Reigeluth, C.M. (2014). The Learner-Centered Paradigm of Education: Roles for Technology. *Educ. Technol., 54*(3), 18-21.

Richert, A., Shehadeh, M., Willicks, F., Jeschke, S. (2016). Digital Transformation of Engineering Education - Empirical Insights from Virtual Worlds and Human-Robot-Collaboration. *Int. J. Eng. Pedagogy (iJEP), 6*(4), 23-29. [iJEP].
[http://dx.doi.org/10.3991/ijep.v6i4.6023]

Sandkuhl, K., Lehmann, H. (2017). *Digital Transformation in higher education-The role of enterprise architectures and portals.* Lecture Notes in Informatics.

Sung, Y.T., Chang, K.E., Liu, T.C. (2016). The effects of integrating mobile devices with teaching and learning on students' learning performance: A meta-analysis and research synthesis. *Comput. Educ., 94*, 252-275.
[http://dx.doi.org/10.1016/j.compedu.2015.11.008]

CHAPTER 2

Digital Transformation in the Education Sector: Benefits and Challenges

Abstract: Students, staff members, and other stakeholders' demands are all shifting rapidly due to advances in electronic technology as well as information analytics. Many of the executives of today are neither tech-savvy nor digital natives, yet they nonetheless recognize the importance of technology in maintaining a competitive edge and fuelling expansion. The study identified many benefits, including facilitating learning and boosting classroom efficiency, facilitating the monitoring of student achievement and growth in the classroom, helping students and teachers work together better, providing unique educational opportunities, increasing efficiency in the classroom and monitoring academic progress. The chapter also identified the following challenges of using DT in the education sector: ineffective digital fixes, uneven availability, developing bad study routines, possible inaccuracies and inability to express oneself. The DT revolution may present some difficulties for institutions, but it is ultimately beneficial to the industry as a whole. It can play a huge role in inspiring both students and educators to adopt cutting-edge methods and outlooks.

Keywords: Benefits, Challenges, Digital transformation, Education sector, Technology.

1. INTRODUCTION

Because of its growing importance in the modern educational framework, information and communication technology (ICT) is a one-of-a-kind mechanical system for any company or country (Nguyen & Luu, 2020). In fact, it is employed as a clever means of communication, one that is perceptive enough to capture the radical alterations in the educational setting and adapt accordingly (Muneer, 2020). As a result, the increasing demand for students' skills and knowledge in the era of globalization has led to a growing interest in incorporating ICT into the classroom. The holistic utilization of technology and human, corporate, and educational drivers guides and supports the digital transformation of instructional processes. To prepare students for the demands of the 4th Industrial Revolution along with other global concerns, such as reducing the negative consequences of climate change by raising public knowledge of its causes and solutions, Education 4.0 emphasizes the development of a wide range of abilities, including critical

Abdul-Mumin Khalid & Obeng Owusu-Boateng
All rights reserved-© 2024 Bentham Science Publishers

thinking, communication, and problem-solving. As much as DT has benefits, it also has limitations. Hence, examining the benefits and challenges for managers of higher education is crucial. The chapter aims to unveil the benefits and challenges of DT in educational settings.

2. LITERATURE

2.1. Benefits of Technology in the Education Sector

The potential technological advances in the classroom are limitless.

• **More Quickly Accessible Data**

Students have access to a wealth of resources, which is one of the greatest benefits of technology in the classroom. At any time and from anywhere, you have access to a wealth of reliable knowledge in the form of websites, tutorial sites, videos on YouTube, e-books, PDFs, and so on (Clarifi Education PBC., 2023). With the introduction of the World Wide Web, kids are seeing the first-ever impact technology has on teaching. Learners' computers, tablets, and mobile phones all have the potential to access vast amounts of data and information with only a few taps or swipes. As a result, you can do things like lesson planning and writing papers alone. Therefore, technology broadens students' horizons and encourages independent study.

• **More Options for Educational Resources**

The internet has made a vast library of educational resources available to students. These resources might be anything from academic publications and papers to online databases and the personal blogs of teachers and authors. If you are in high school, you will find these to be really helpful. If you have all the relevant data, facts, and figures on hand, you will have an easier time writing academic papers. A student's work can benefit from using the available facts to back up an argument, prove a hypothesis, or arrive at the right conclusion. There is no need to exert an inordinate amount of effort while using technology to improve students' academic performance (Clarifi Education PBC., 2023).

• **Expands Opportunities for Study at a Distance**

The ability to study from afar is a major perk of the Internet for students. With the advent of the internet, distance learning has become a viable option. Through the use of a computer screen or online discussion forum, students can acquire the same knowledge. During a virtual meeting, students from the same university can exchange files, links, and information. Traditional classroom time is being supplemented with online instruction, and the result is improved student performance in both contexts. They supplement the education of kids, especially the weaker ones, by attending classes outside of school hours online. Furthermore, students who are interested in pursuing their passions in areas like Data Analytics that are not included in the standard school curriculum can do so by enrolling in an appropriate online course. Other emerging educational institutions provide purely online courses in a wide range of disciplines and professions. Some of the most well-known places to take extensive online classes are Coursera, edX, and Udemy.

• Modify Educational Practices

One of EdTech's many advantages is that it makes teaching simpler for everyone involved. Teachers have the option of working with students remotely or coordinating extracurricular activities. This improves their teaching skills, aids student learning, and ultimately leads to higher test scores (Clarifi Education PBC., 2022). Also, because of the widespread use of mobile and desktop apps, pupils now have access to digital attention coaches. They assist educators in keeping track of students' assignments (Clarifi Education PBC., 2023) and facilitating classroom management. They can monitor pupils' progress on assignments and alert them if they are running late. To monitor and help their kids' academic progress, many schools and teachers today use Internet resources. They can quickly see who is struggling academically or who is falling behind. They can help guide them in the right direction and aid in their academic progress.

• Boosts Students' Ability to Communicate in the Classroom

This is a significant advantage of modern technology for universities. Higher-level students improve their communication skills through exposure to numerous technological resources and online learning opportunities. Many students feel uncomfortable raising their hands or talking to professors in front of their peers. Yet, they can open up and participate fully in online meetings and lectures (Clarifi Education PBC., 2023) despite their usual shyness and reserve. During their separate periods in front of the screen, they can engage in any form of digital communication they like. Students who want to succeed in school and their careers in the future must have strong communication skills. Better communication skills allow students to articulate their ideas and contribute meaningfully to class discussions.

• Makes Learning Entertaining

Young children are notoriously difficult to corral into a classroom setting. They have a short attention span. Similarly, it can be difficult for older pupils to maintain concentration long enough to finish a particularly substantial paper or project. In general, school is a dreary experience for most kids. But because of technological advancements, it has become something that anyone can enjoy (Clarifi Education PBC., 2022). Students are more engaged in class because of the usage of technology like tablets, laptops, VR/AR gadgets, and touchscreen boards. Teachers will have no trouble maintaining their students' interests. In a similar vein, these cutting-edge tools aid college-level learners' comprehension of difficult scientific concepts and theoretical frameworks through interactive, hands-on experiences. In this way, the fact that kids enjoy utilizing technology in the classroom is one of its most salient advantages. As a result of their increased engagement, pupils begin performing better in the classroom.

- **Facilitates the Development of Student's Abilities and Knowledge**

Students can acquire new abilities and expand their knowledge thanks to the incorporation of technology into the classroom. The web and distance learning programs make it doable. Those with an insatiable thirst for knowledge have access to an unprecedented wealth of resources online. They will be able to put their newfound expertise to use in the classroom, which will help them achieve better results (Clarifi Education PBC., 2023) than their peers. Education technology is also assisting bright young minds in acquiring marketable abilities. Business analytics, machine learning, data science, and digital marketing are just some examples of professional abilities that are not typically taught in the classroom. If you want to learn a new skill outside of school hours, you can do so by enrolling in an online course. A student can learn the material thoroughly and prepare for a future in a specific vocation.

- **Helps Pupils Remain Abreast of Developments in the Technology World**

Students greatly benefit from digital learning since it allows them to keep up with the rapid pace of technological change. Students can easily implement them, resulting in improved education for your students. Digital technologies such as task managers, online lecture halls, and e-learning apps are becoming increasingly popular. You can help your students succeed in school by keeping up with the latest developments in educational technology (EdTech). Those who keep up with the latest developments in educational technology have a better chance of finding employment (Clarifi Education PBC., 2023) in the future. They can aid businesses in running more smoothly and more quickly, thanks to their familiarity with cutting-edge tech and trends.

- **Helps Students Improve their Emotional Health**

Students' emotional and physiological well-being is boosted by the use of digital tools in the classroom. Their boring classes are made more manageable and engaging with the use of a variety of digital tools (Clarifi Education PBC., 2023) for students. There are numerous ways in which the use of EdTech might boost students' mental abilities. Two major factors are virtual classrooms and the adoption of augmented reality. They improve a student's capacity for reading, understanding, learning, memory, thought, and logic. All of them have a significant effect on students' ability to learn and their grades. When students use technology in the classroom to improve their academic performance, it boosts their self-esteem and motivation. This improves students' emotional well-being and allows them to focus more intently on their schoolwork.

- **Facilitates Learning and Boosts Classroom Efficiency**

The benefits of EdTech extend beyond the classroom and improve the instructors' work as well. Teachers can improve their lesson delivery with the aid of technological tools, including audio-visual presentations, virtual classrooms, wide-screen projectors, and digital planners. In turn, pupils benefit from an increase in their level of understanding and comprehension as a result (Clarifi Education PBC., 2023). Besides, technology boosts educators' efficiency. Students are more invested in their education and have access to additional learning possibilities because of the use of digital tools. Many educators can use differentiated strategies and materials to help their pupils who are struggling. Overall, children and schools benefit from teachers' increased efficiency made possible by technological advancements in education.

- **Facilitates the Monitoring of Student Achievement and Growth in the Classroom**

The assignment management system or planner that teachers use is a great example of how technology has improved education. They are electronic versions of traditional school planners and diaries. All homework and class projects for a given day, week, or month can be entered by the teachers. Time limits can be set by them. They are kept up to date in real-time as students begin, pause, and finish assignments. Teachers can see their pupils' progress as a whole with the dashboard that comes standard on most digital planners. They may observe how much time is spent studying, what assignments are done, what marks are earned, and so on (Clarifi Education PBC., 2022). Student's strengths and weaknesses, as well as their overall progress, can be monitored in this way. They can use this information to plan out their curriculum for the next class more effectively.

• Minimizes the Impact of Outside Disturbances

Although some authorities have suggested that educational technology is a distraction, the contrary appears to be true. However, this can only be guaranteed if teachers and schools are adept at making use of technology. Students are easily sidetracked by mobile learning apps hence they should not be made available. (Clarifi Education PBC., 2023) They frequently switch to using other forms of online entertainment. Therefore, select instructional aids, such as desktop digital planners, that enable pupils to concentrate on their studies with minimal disruption. These apps are designed to help students focus on their studies by isolating them from the outside world.

• Helps Students and Teachers Work Together Better

Using technology in the classroom is a surefire way to make learning more interactive for both students and instructors. Asynchronous communication between instructors and students is only one benefit of using an online learning system. It also promotes student-teacher connections on a personal level. By staying at home, students can upload their projects or homework for their teachers to review and provide feedback on. Group projects that require students to work together can be compared to the experiences students will have in a traditional classroom and an online learning environment. Students work in small groups to complete assignments given by their teacher. Some kids will be disruptive, others will offer questions, yet others will be too shy, and still, others will not get a chance to speak. In contrast, this is not the case with online courses (Clarifi Education PBC., 2023) for obvious reasons. In a virtual classroom, every single student has access to the network. Each student has a screen on which the teacher addresses and resolves their questions and concerns. It is fair to say that students are more likely to communicate with one another outside of the classroom thanks to online learning. They can help each other out with challenging undertakings by pooling their knowledge and resources.

• Unique Educational Opportunities

Thanks to advancements in technology, kids now have access to a wealth of learning materials around the clock. Those who struggle to understand the material presented in class have the option of attending additional virtual meetings with a tutor (Clarifi Education PBC., 2023) to help them catch up. To be more specific, educators can now design individualized lesson plans for their students. Having the ability to focus on each student is a major perk of online education. They also have the opportunity to study in an atmosphere that best suits them. They need not look around at or imitate their classmates. They can instead complete their work according to the teacher's strict timetable.

- **Increase in Efficiency in the Classroom**

Students' increased academic output is a direct result of the increased use of online learning resources. EdTech provides them with opportunities for both individualized instruction and the growth of critical thinking and time management abilities. In higher classes, this becomes increasingly important. It helps them stay on top of their many tasks and finish each one in due time without being overwhelmed. Online courses with strict deadlines have been shown to instill a sense of responsibility in their students (Clarifi Education PBC., 2023). They become experts at sticking to their study schedules and avoiding interruptions. In addition, materials and tools for education are readily available to students at any time. And if they need more guidance on an assignment outside of class, they can start a conversation with a teacher online. Therefore, there is no need to worry about being stranded on a task. As a whole, students can devote more time and effort to their studies with the aid of online learning resources.

- **Inspiring Students with Gaming (Gamification)**

It is no surprise that technology stimulates originality and fresh ideas. Developers of various educational technologies used entertaining features to further capture the attention of young students. Apps that provide such feedback on the successful completion of a learning step are said to be "gamified". Such feedback can take the form of points, scores, clap noises, visual congratulations, gratitude messages, and so on. The accumulation of virtual coins, gems, or other incentives is a common feature of many eLearning apps' interactive game aspects. They have individual scoreboards so that students can compare their performance to that of their peers and strive to do better. To rephrase the claim made by Clarify Education PBC., 2023, "Gamification helped students learn in a fun and interesting way by building focus and encouraging them to do better."

- **Monitoring Academic Progress**

Teachers' access to performance data is a potent tool for improving education. They can use this data to track student development and provide constructive criticism. But not only educators can benefit from the knowledge, students can keep tabs on their progress in real time and evaluate where they excel and where they could use improvement with the use of tracking technology. By using it for self-evaluation, students can strengthen their approach to learning (McGregor, 2021). Students can take immediate, actionable steps to improve their performance without having to wait for instructor comments, thanks to the tracking technology that is now available. Students can become autonomous in their learning and make well-informed decisions thanks to the data provided by performance monitoring systems.

- **Analysis of Data**

Information can be used to make schools more efficient and responsive to kids' needs. It allows us to shift from a rigidly standardized model of education to one that is more responsive to individual student's needs (McGregor, 2021). It is easier to learn when information and tools are consolidated. It makes it easier to keep an eye on how things are done behind the scenes. This allows for the evaluation of pedagogical, instructional, and other related approaches. This makes it simpler to pinpoint issues and implement solutions that boost productivity.

- **Infinite Resources**

Education is accessible to all with the use of technology in the classroom. A wide range of materials is made available to all students (McGregor, 2021). In addition, when extended reality will grow, the classroom's walls will disappear. It paves the way for experiences like virtual science simulations using high-priced professional equipment and virtual tours to any time and place that would otherwise be inaccessible to students. They make it possible for students to actively engage with and retain more information from course materials.

- **Future-oriented Education**

The pace at which technology is changing every sector of the economy is accelerating. The education system cannot afford to remain stagnant and teach in the same outmoded ways. Only *via* digital transformation can students acquire the cutting-edge technology skills necessary for professional success (McGregor, 2021). Every industry seems to discover a new use for things like robotics, AI, VR, electronics, telecommunications, and automation. Therefore, today's educational programs need to incorporate the use of digital resources and ensure that their pupils acquire the appropriate knowledge and abilities. This is the only way to ensure a sustainable educational system.

- **Experiential Learning**

The concepts of virtual reality and augmented reality allow for more immersive learning experiences, which, in turn, serve to increase students' understanding. These tools were utilized by educators to help pupils better understand complex scientific concepts, perplexing theories, and historical locations. Compared to textbooks, this help pupils better understand and retain the material (Clarifi Education PBC., 2023). Technology in the classroom has also greatly increased kids' enthusiasm for learning. Books no longer have a monopoly on the information that students absorb. They have access to video and audio content, as well as the ability to conduct web searches. They are able to learn more about the topic, thus, their papers are more in-depth, and they earn higher grades as a result.

• Assist Academics and Pupils

Artificial intelligence (AI) provides for the automation of a wide variety of mundane jobs, including grading. The chatbot is prepared to respond to the most frequently asked questions that educators face daily. Neural networks may evaluate the efficacy of previously taught courses, provide recommendations for course content and resources, and inform instructors about gaps in their lesson plans.

• Reduces Anxiety for Busy Parents and Educators

Teachers no longer have to keep a journal or checklist of responsibilities thanks to digital tools. Teachers can save a lot of time thanks to online tools like lesson planning calendars, grading apps, and tests. The parents can also breathe a sigh of relief thanks to this. Students can use a variety of applications to keep track of their work and be reminded of upcoming due dates. Therefore, kids develop a sense of agency and get their work done on schedule. Parents do not have to stand over their children's shoulders to make sure they are studying (Clarifi Education PBC., 2023), thanks to this technology.

• Remove Prejudice from Evaluations

Teachers need to spend a significant amount of time checking and grading student work. But because people are not always objective, pupils' marks do not necessarily reflect how much they have learned. By replacing subjective evaluation with objective AI, we can solve this issue and free up time for educators to spend with pupils.

• Invests in Tomorrow's Digital World

Learning with technology now will help students succeed in a world that will soon be entirely digital. In the future, technology will permeate every aspect of life, if not directly power it (Clarifi Education PBC., 2023). Students are introduced to cutting-edge tools through the use of EdTech resources like virtual classrooms, AI-assisted planners, video learning, engaged learning for TV applications, online exams, *etc.* It also aids them in prioritizing how they use technology. They can tell the difference between learning technologies and entertainment technologies like video games, television applications, over-the-top (OTT) services, social networking, *etc.* Because of this, they will be able to set limits on their technology use (Kyriazi, 2015).

• Allows for Long-term Education

EdTech's contribution to environmental preservation and long-term education is among its most important advantages. Teachers are pushing students to take examinations online or create homework on computers, which might be shared *via* email or cloud storage, resulting in a significant reduction in the amount of paper used. In light of rising environmental degradation, many schools and educators are switching from paper books to eReaders (Clarifi Education PBC., 2023). The importance of environmental sustainability is not lost on today's kids because of the role technology has played in the classroom. Learning through electronic and digital mediums is beneficial for both the environment and the convenience of instructors and students. It is a boon to their budgets for things like textbooks, binders, whiteboards, planners, field trips, and other educational necessities.

• Convenience

Incorporating ICT into the educational process has been shown to improve both proficiency and accessibility. Based on the agreed-upon schedule and due date, students can complete their online examinations at any time. Learning online eliminates the need for students to meet in person. Asynchronous processing is possible (Pokhrel & Chhetri, 2021; Wei *et al.*, 2022).

• Allows each Learner to Get Through the Material at their Rate

Children can learn at their own pace because of the incorporation of technology into classrooms. Many kids have weaker memorization or comprehension skills than others. They struggle to keep up in a traditional classroom setting and can not benefit from the standard techniques of instruction. They require individualized instruction to improve their academic performance (Clarifi Education PBC., 2023). The use of technology in the classroom has benefited these pupils greatly because it has allowed for a more individualized learning experience. Teachers can now provide their students with personalized lesson plans and schedules *via* educational applications. Depending on their expertise and availability, they can assign tasks and establish deadlines for completion. Many children can benefit from this, and their grades and test scores all can rise as a result. It helps educators find effective ways to instruct pupils who struggle with attention deficit hyperactivity disorder (ADHD) and related conditions.

• Collaboration for Education

Digital education necessitates group work. Learning management systems allow teachers to create and manage classes online. Google Docs, Twiddla, Edmodo, and similar shared creative platforms facilitate co-authors' papers and presentations. Companies are already making use of such interactive tools (Sinku, 2021).

- **Personnel Selection and Management**

Colleges and universities, more specifically, have a responsibility to attract and engage with the families of their prospective students. They need a website, social media accounts, and an actual brochure, as well as open houses and other events, to be visible on the platforms these audiences utilize (Al-Shakarchi, 2022). To meet these and other demands, full digital transformation of all processes is necessary (Al-Shakarchi, 2022). Comparably, technology can revolutionize the management of the organization's activities, many of which may have previously relied on manual and paper-based methods. One such example would be replacing in-person communication with kids and guardians with text messages or email instead of a phone call or letter.

- **Curriculums Geared Toward the Future**

A school offers courses on futuristic topics such as robots, AI, automation, and science fiction. Although there is mounting evidence that workforce requirements will shift and grow substantially in the years ahead, the business lacks the resources to adequately train its employees (Majeed, 2023; Sinku, 2021). Developing and improving the revised curricula will not take decades. Students now have easier access to timely and relevant information. The ability to rapidly update and function depends on having constant access to new information and tools.

- **AI Tutoring Provides Extra Help for College Students**

Teachers in universities obviously cannot be there for their students 24 hours a day, 7 days a week. However, no single student has the intellectual capacity to absorb everything they encounter in their studies without the aid of a tutor. The AI tutors can offer this supplementary help. Several different AI-powered tutoring applications are available now, and they may assist kids with the fundamentals of math, writing, and other topics.

- **Availability of State-of-the-art Resources**

The rapid growth of blended learning in recent years can be directly attributed to the widespread use of digital learning tools and their ease of use (Majeed, 2023; Malthora, 2020). Blended learning courses have been shown to improve student outcomes compared to either traditional face-to-face or online courses (Majeed, 2023; Smith & Hill, 2019).

• Strengthens the Partnership Between Home and School

When parents are invested in their children's education, it has been shown to improve their children's academic performance and overall health. Parents are encouraged to be involved in their child's education by receiving electronic progress reports and remarks *via* automation systems. Envision a software program that effectively guides students toward a career path that best suits their unique set of skills and interests (Sinku, 2021).

• Instruction and Evaluation

EdTech, or educational technology, creates dynamic classrooms in the form of VLEs or learning management systems (LMSs). These cutting-edge web-based hubs offer students more than simply a centralized location to store and retrieve digital content. Online grading and assessment of student work are made easier and take less time with the help of this learning platform (Al-Shakarchi, 2022). Teachers' workloads can be reduced while still meeting the needs of their students by using video and audio-recorded feedback with annotations that specify exactly where feedback is applicable. Students are better able to make connections between concepts and think creatively when they can tag additional course information in their feedback. The best learning environments are those in which instructors use a pedagogical approach that combines online and in-person instruction. Whether a student is physically located at a school, at home, or elsewhere, the online platform can serve as a learning environment (Al-Shakarchi, 2022). Some educators now use technology to implement a 'flipped' classroom model, in which students are given access to lectures or reading materials outside of class and then return for in-person discussion and practice of the material.

• Monitoring of Academic Progress

One effect of the digital transformation on education is a more accurate method of gauging pupils' progress. Technology can play a crucial role in recording data from students' projects, allowing educators and parents to monitor student's progress over time (Sinku, 2021). Manuals or creative works, for instance, might be compared at regular intervals to previously recorded digital content, allowing for a more precise assessment of strengths and weaknesses.

- **Internet**

Students are more motivated to study hard at their schoolwork because of improved Internet access made possible by digitization. There is evidence that India's educational system is adapting to the modern world (Sharma, 2020).

- **Data Analysis Yields Better Results**

Analytic tools can be used in schools for progress monitoring and improvement. By analyzing the data collected, teachers can better cater their lessons to the needs of their students (Sinku, 2021). It will be easier to catch up in a course if you can figure out why a student did not show up for a certain term. We will be able to make far more accurate diagnoses of these problems with the help of modern technology.

- **E-library**

Since traditional libraries have become obsolete, e-library digitalization aids in establishing e-libraries by providing PC labs in educational institutions (Sharma, 2020). It helps eliminate problems that crop up over the course of the study.

- **Interaction**

The same ways in which digital is appropriate for recruitment and administration are also possible during the learning process. Students and teachers can talk in real time regardless of their physical locations, thanks to online discussion boards and live video interactions (Al-Shakarchi, 2022). Students can work together and exchange resources online to learn from one another and from established best practices.

- **Distant Education**

In today's era of widespread digitization, students typically choose what is now called correspondence courses, which are delivered *via* the Internet. The course outline and other information can be mailed to students. We owe a debt of gratitude to technological progress for making a variety of classes at a given level more accessible than ever before (Sharma, 2020).

- **Measurement**

Learners' performance and development can be closely tracked with the help of data. Decisions may be made with more precision, and students at risk can be identified before it is too late. Then, educators can take corrective measures to bring kids back on track as soon as possible (Al-Shakarchi, 2022).

• Online Training

If a school or university does not have the funds to send its students on field trips, those students still have the option of participating in curriculum-related online activities. Educators who use online platforms should encourage their students to exercise caution by allowing them to leave comments and participate in surveys (Sharma, 2020). Students' active participation in workshops is required, and workshops should encourage two-way communication.

2.1.1. Challenges of DT in the Education Sector

• Nothing will Ever Change Under this System

The unpreparedness of the current system for changes is the most typical issue with the digital transformation in higher education. Both the internal training program and the staff are affected by this. This calls for a measured approach to digitization, with regular checks on progress toward goals and the efficacy of implemented changes.

• Not Being Hired

Lack of onboarding is a potential threat to the efficiency and success of digitization in institutions of higher learning. New digital tools introduced as part of digitalization initiatives should be made available to staff and students, and appropriate training should be provided. In that case, these resources would be useless.

• Too Rapid or too Slow of a Shift

As we have already mentioned, it is important to take the transition to digital methods in higher education slowly. You should not rush to bring everything that happens offline into the online world, adopt every digital technology at once, or make every process change at once. Do not put off upgrading to more modern equipment.

• Transformation to Digital Technology Requires Education

Training that begins at a young age has the most impact. High school education, for instance, will provide superior preparation for college. Learning outcomes are influenced by students' levels of engagement. Superior intelligence calls for exemplary behavior and skill. Students should practice skills like self-directed study, knowledge retrieval, and evaluation in the context of the natural sciences. Therefore, all educators must work together to ensure the best possible educational experience for their students. It is crucial to supplement the learning activities with specialized classes. Assessing the learning process is essential for evaluating the outcomes of online education (Lile & Bran, 2014). To finish the teacher's evaluation, students must first complete a self-assessment and a peer-review assessment (Santos et al., 2016).

- **Not Having a Plan**

Any company can fail due to a lack of planning. The first step in implementing digital transformation in higher education should be to develop a plan (Polych, 2023) to guide your efforts; explain in detail what needs to change, why it needs to change, what dangers or difficulties might arise as a result, what solutions might be implemented, *etc.* You can organize the digitization process qualitatively when you have a firm grasp of the way forward.

- **Ineffective Digital Fix**

The educational sector now has access to a wide variety of digital resources. However, it is unclear if they will be able to assist you. Simply incorporating digital solutions into your system will not produce the desired outcome. These options should be of sufficient quality to fulfill your specifications. Consulting experts and coming up with your solutions is your best bet.

- **Partners and Contractors with Little Experience**

You need to make sure the team you hire to create the correct tools for you has the necessary expertise and experience. During the digital transition in higher education, many educational institutions have to deal with the issue of hiring contractors without sufficient experience. Therefore, you should consider the team's track record, portfolio, client testimonials, *etc.*, when making a recruiting decision. If you try to work with a group of people who lack the necessary expertise, you will be disappointed. Unfortunately, not all educators have received adequate preparation to use the increasingly sophisticated machinery in their classrooms. As a result, students are not learning anything from their technological experiences. Using science and technology in education is a positive thing, but it will take some time for this theoretical knowledge to be translated into a practical set of abilities (Sharma, 2020).

- **Uneven Availability**

Not every student can afford cutting-edge equipment due to its high price tag (Vial, 2019). This is why a uniform approach to equipping classrooms with the technology and resources pupils require is critical to the success of the digital revolution as a whole. On the other side, educators need not transform education at the student level but can focus on tools for the whole class (Sinku, 2021).

- **Developing bad Study Routines**

One's study habits suffer when overly dependent on electronic devices. Many students look online for the easiest answers to their math homework instead of putting in the time and effort required to truly master the material. There will be a limitless number of misspelled words in written work because of spell checkers.

- **Possible Inaccuracies**

It was humanity that created technological advancements, not the other way around. Just as humans are not perfect, neither is technology (Raja, 2018). The irritation of both students and teachers might result from technical difficulties that slow down the learning process, such as server errors and connectivity issues (Sharma, 2020). Every minute spent in class or at a learning institution is precious thus none of it must be wasted on unimportant problems.

- **Subpar Material**

With the rapid progress of technology, website owners are under increasing pressure to improve their sites' search engine ranks at the expense of the quality of their content. As a result of careless copying and pasting from other sites, many websites present inaccurate information. As a result, students are being misled by incorrect data found on these sites (Papagiannidis et al., 2020). These may end up being significant roadblocks in their growth.

- **Web Surfing**

It is a subset of the wider digital divide issue. The number of people who may participate in digital education and the kind of materials available are both impacted by the availability of the Internet. Despite the popularity of cell phones, broadband Internet is still difficult to come by and often prohibitively expensive in many rural regions (Balkin & Sonnevend, 2016). Many students in the world may not have adequate access to digital education since it relies heavily on video and multimedia programming that consumes a lot of bandwidth; if they only have low-bandwidth access, they will have to rely mostly on text-based systems.

- **Inability to Express Oneself**

Some worry that individuals are losing their social skills and their capacity to communicate with one another as a result of all the new technology (Sharma, 2020). There are legitimate worries regarding the loss of interpersonal and collaboration skills that children generally gain inside a classroom setting as a result of the widespread adoption of new technologies designed for individual usage.

- **The Foundations of Technology**

To begin, a switch to digital learning necessitates a retooling of the whole educational system, from students to teachers, administrators and policymakers. Apps and platforms for learning and administration at every level come pre-installed on the hardware we use today. If the use of information technology in schools typically refers to discrete applications, then digital transformation necessitates that all these components work together and are available from inside the same interface. Everything from lesson planning and delivery to student and teacher communication is made possible by this platform. For this platform to function properly, a reliable Internet connection is required (Osam, 2021). The amount of socioeconomic growth in any given area is strongly correlated with the rate of progress toward a fully digital society. As a result, education cannot just do it alone; it needs help from, and cooperation with, other fields. Since they are used to doing things on their own, this can be a huge obstacle.

- **Competence and Acumen in Management**

Naturally, the educational mindset and the administrative skills of school administrators would need to evolve for such a system to function effectively. They need to figure out how to successfully utilize technology to capture what is possible in cyberspace. To both grasp technology and recognize its limitations, they must be equipped with knowledge and a digital mindset. In addition, the context is also important for digital transformation. There is no one-size-fits-all approach to methods and transition; instead, business leaders will need to create their own strategy, solutions, and transformation roadmap based on their unique circumstances and as little as possible on the examples set by other businesses or by those in other nations (Osam, 2021).

- **Competence with Technological Tools**

If educators are not equipped to make effective use of digital tools, the transition will fail. If teachers and students do not interact in person, it is important for them to be able to put themselves in the shoes of the students so they can understand and respect what they are going through (Osam, 2021). Naturally, they need the help of technical staff and technology experts at all times to make sure that instruction runs well. Teachers also require updated abilities to manage their classrooms and keep pupils engaged in meaningful work. They have the most significant role in determining the success of digital transformation initiatives and online training programs. Almost no one with IT experience works in a traditional school. However, technicians are in high demand instead of administrative staff members due to the widespread adoption of online education (Osam, 2021). Schools can always find a way to contact this workout, but budget priorities shift frequently, necessitating the implementation of governance and financial management procedures.

- **The Ability of the Student**

Due to the delay in starting the 2019-2020 academic year caused by the COVID-19 pandemic, we polled college professors and undergraduates on their "readiness for online learning". Learners are far less prepared for online education than teachers, according to the survey results. Seventy-six percent or more of the students polled (from various departments and numerous cities and provinces) are not prepared for online education. There are issues not only because of technical factors such as telecommunication equipment and infrastructure but also because of the lecturers' tactics and techniques, which have failed to convince the students. Online learning requires students to have the right mindset, knowledge, and support to be successful. They also require guidance on how to make the most of their time studying online (Osam, 2021).

- **Education Disparities**

Since the internet is accessible from anywhere at any time, many people believe that this will lead to "digital equity" (digital equity) in educational opportunities. This has the potential to exacerbate existing disparities in educational opportunities between geographical areas and children from varying socioeconomic backgrounds (Osam, 2021). Students in rural or mountainous places without reliable Internet access will struggle to gain access to not only advanced pedagogical materials but even the most fundamental ones.

- **Authority over Design Patterns and Technical Standards**

Technology standards and platforms for creating and displaying content, as well as supporting communication and interaction between students and instructors, are essential in online education, especially when dealing with multimedia (Balkin & Sonnevend, 2016). Questions regarding the design of these platforms and standards include whether or not they are proprietary and need licensing fees, whether or not they are compatible with other platforms and standards, and whether or not they are freely open for use by others. With universally accepted standards, it is simple to transfer data and content from one system to another. Moving educational resources or exchanging information (such as homework, collaborative projects, grades, and evaluations) between platforms will be challenging if they are not compatible. This may reduce free-riding competition, but it will also encourage lock-in. By contrast, locked standards will not only offer internet businesses more power but will also discourage third-party development.

- **Compatibility with Existing Systems**

Most businesses and institutions in the modern world rely on technologically oriented systems and infrastructures to run efficiently and effectively every day. Noncompliance with new digital technology to progress educational systems is a major issue holding back digital transformation. Because of this incompatibility, it will be necessary to either upgrade, alter, or replace the existing integration system, which will take time and money.

- **Language**

The barrier to education is no longer location-based but linguistic. As long as learners can comprehend the language of teaching, schools can attract students from all corners of the globe. To compete in international markets, it will be necessary for online businesses to provide multilingual options (Balkin & Sonnevend, 2016). Businesses often choose to prioritize the most widely spoken languages like English, Chinese, Arabic, and Spanish to save money. This trend may help these languages become even more dominant in the future. The rise of a dominant national language through digital education can have unintended consequences for minority languages.

- **Resistance to Alteration**

The next important steps toward digital maturity are rejected by some major policymakers. People like to get used to their routines and are reluctant to try new things, both of which are detrimental to their personal development and evolution (Omer, 2018). Many educators, however, are afraid to adapt to changing technological, cultural, and mental frameworks for fear of failing and thus not learning anything new. There are other problems with EdTech, but this is the most important one. Not everyone in the education system is on board with embracing technology. They believe that education is most efficient when it occurs in real time, such as in a school setting or through direct instruction from a parent. One of the fundamental issues that impede digital transformation is a lack of motivation to adapt to technology-based methods. Fear of failure and a lack of drive to learn contribute to people's reluctance to try new things and step outside their comfort zones, according to research (McGregor, 2021). In addition to increasing the digital maturity of all parties involved, digital transformation calls for intensive efforts to promote shifts in perspective and organizational culture.

- **Lack of Planning**

The absence of a holistic plan is also a serious problem. The term "digital transformation" encompasses a wide variety of shifts on many fronts. It may take longer to reach the goal and reap the anticipated benefits if an educational institution does not outline the step-by-step process of transformation for its particular scenario (McGregor, 2021). Therefore, an organization needs to articulate the benefits of digital transformation and clearly define the outcome it seeks. It must also carefully map out the transition and figure out how to minimize disruptions for both kids and staff.

- **The Missing Link in Digital Education**

Adopting digital methods calls for competent computer users. All education industry workers need to be skilled for the transition to go smoothly. Employers should encourage workers to expand their knowledge of technology by providing training and other chances (McGregor, 2021). Teachers and school leaders can be equipped to take advantage of digital transformation by participating in professional development opportunities such as workshops, seminars, lectures, and online courses.

- **Free-form Information**

While data is essential for digital transformation, many academic institutions store it in a fragmented and chaotic fashion. Incomplete or incorrect information can no longer be relied upon. It can lead to confusion and bad choices in administrative and educational processes. Therefore, organizations miss out on the opportunities presented by digital transitions, particularly in the realm of data analytics. Institutions need to find technologies for reliable data collection, efficient usage, and secure storage to integrate data from multiple sources into a single useful resource (McGregor, 2021).

- **Constant Updates**

Constant improvements to technology are required. Whatever educational resources and software are used, continuous updates are essential for schools, students, and educators. Because of this, they have extra work to do to keep up with the latest developments in educational technology, such as checking for and installing software updates, upgrading hardware, purchasing new gadgets, *etc*.

- **Having Less-than-ideal Expertise**

To propel innovation within the company, there must be sufficient levels of trust, expertise, and talent. To ensure a seamless and efficient digital conversion, educational institutions must compete for a limited pool of talent or adopt innovative techniques for upgrading rising players using cloud infrastructure (Arnab Kundu et al., 2018).

• **Cost Increases**

There are always financial considerations when implementing new technology. Educators and students alike are compelled to spend money on new gadgets and EdTech solutions to keep up with the rapidly evolving educational technology landscape. The use of eLearning, or technology in education, is increasing the price of education.

• **Probability of Success**

As a result of the proliferation of digital resources, educators and corporate trainers now have access to a wealth of metrics that reveal important information about their students and clients. To sum up, the level of specificity provided is priceless. The issue is that these data are uniform, inconsistent, and unreliable, especially in the field of education. The ability to obtain flowing, rapid, reliable, and structured data is dependent on educational leaders making educated forecasts, integrating business decisions, and implementing new educational measures to grasp the most relevant and enlightening data (Omer, 2018).

• **Lack of Technical Knowledge**

Teachers and students alike are expected to possess a foundational understanding of technology. They are the ones who benefit the most from using educational technology. Therefore, they must possess or acquire the knowledge and abilities necessary to make the most of educational technology.

• **Scalability**

Some aspects of schooling, as we have seen, scale well when done online, while others are likely to be time-consuming and expensive to implement. Digital educational businesses will thrive if they can find ways to reduce the expense of or altogether avoid supplying these labor-intensive features. If digital businesses are relieved of the obligation (and cost) of providing the time-consuming components of education, they will do so.

• **The Provision of means or Facilities**

Video streaming, online chat, video calling, and so on are internet-dependent features that must be built into any EdTech application or device. Any Edtech app or tool requires a stable connection to the internet with sufficient speed and a device that can run it. Therefore, schools, educators, and students require these materials.

- **Not having a Plan**

Knowing how and where to begin the digital transformation in any given field or company is one of today's greatest obstacles to development. The uncertainty of a widespread shift makes it hard to choose the best course of action or formulate an effective strategy.

- **When it comes to Teaching Children, "Digital First" is the only Option**

Learning is still learning. The primary goals of digital education remain the same: to foster talent, to test students' thinking, to introduce them to novel concepts, and to encourage them to develop their creative solutions to problems. The tools we employ to facilitate that must always come second. It is tempting to think of digital education as requiring a clean slate, but in reality, educational institutions should build their transformation efforts on their greatest asset: their teaching expertise. Online or offline, the fundamentals of good teaching have not changed.

- **Education Spending Constraints**

Two-thirds of low and lower-middle-income countries are expected to see a rise in their education financing gaps, which will hurt the already meager resources available to maintain current levels of education service provision (World Bank, 2021). Meanwhile, it is predicted that US$200 billion in additional funds per year are needed to universalize digital learning in low and lower-middle-income countries (UNICEF, 2021b). While nearly all high-income countries invested in digital remote learning as part of their response to the epidemic, barely a quarter of low-income countries did so.

- **Lack of Personnel and Resources for Tracking the Progress of Educational Programs**

When it comes to monitoring student progress and tailoring ICT interventions, many nations are woefully unprepared (UNESCO & UNICEF, 2021b). This is connected to the system's ability to track associated metrics like student retention, educator readiness, and assessment of student learning. The government's ability to plan and alter its responses was hampered by a lack of disaggregated data on which children were using remote and digital learning possibilities during the pandemic.

• An Increase in Internet Dangers, Privacy, and Safety

The COVID-19 pandemic exacerbated a growing problem: kids are spending more time online and engaging digitally, putting them at more risk of cybercrime, cyberbullying, and privacy and data ownership violations (End Violence Against Children, 2020). Digital learning strategies should also take into account the fact that students' mental health and feelings of isolation worsened as a result of distance learning during the pandemic (Malolos et al., 2021; UNESCO & UNICEF, 2021a). It is common knowledge that cutting-edge gadgets do not come cheap. The high price tag associated with this type of technology makes it prohibitive for most public schools to implement it. Parents may find this challenging because their children may develop a dependence on devices that are not available at home (Sharma, 2020).

• Rapid Results in Digital Transformation are Possible

The rapid pace of change in education in 2020 has been noted by nearly all service providers, including us. However, businesses must not fall for the myth that they can achieve digital literacy fast. To quickly adapt from brick-and-mortar to digital sales, it can be useful to begin with off-the-shelf solutions. However, companies must never lose sight of the fact that, behind all the data and machinery, there are actual people with specific requirements. A lecture can be recorded on video and uploaded to the web in a short amount of time. Digital education does not include merely attending classes or taking tests online (Medina, 2023) nevertheless. The experience needs to be considerably more comprehensive, with content designed to encourage interaction and participation in a digital setting. Building an immersive digital world is not a quick or inexpensive process, but it is well worth the effort.

• Risk

Students may be hesitant to fully embrace the online classroom because of poor content or insufficient support. Teachers may have trouble developing useful digital lessons if they are not adequately trained. The performance or compatibility of novel technological solutions is uncertain (Medina, 2023) and may not live up to expectations. The potential benefits of digital education are substantial, but we must be prepared to foresee obstacles and adjust our strategies in response to customer input.

• The Reach of Digital Education is Unmatched

Naturally, digital education has enormous potential to expand access to learning and help more students than ever before. However, one must use caution and care before diving headfirst into massive undertakings. It is crucial to test new ideas before chasing volume since, as we have seen, digital change carries inherent risks. Test out cutting-edge features, poll your students for input, refine your approach and your tools, and try again (Medina, 2023). Then and only then can digital education be scaled to meet demand. Even if there are no obvious logistical hurdles to admitting more students, it is vital to keep in mind that enrollment can still be constrained by other factors. Each of our schools caters to a certain group of students who share their knowledge, experience, interests, and resources. While digital may enable previously impossible levels of scalability, we need to be mindful of what can be accomplished without watering down the quality of our programs or our faculty's credentials and standing in the community.

• **Management of Creative Works**

There is a wealth of knowledge that can be accessed online for no cost or at a low cost, thanks to the Creative Commons license. Existing institutions already make use of this content to augment their courses, and conversely, some educational institutions make their lectures and course materials available to the general public. Some online businesses rely heavily on open educational resources. However, intellectual property will be essential in the long run, as it is in many other fields of knowledge creation. Many of the most useful resources for education will have their use restricted by licenses, making them unavailable to for-profit and non-profit businesses and organizations.

• **Worse in some Instances**

For pupils already struggling to keep up academically, the digital divide just makes matters worse. The remote and digital learning possibilities available during the pandemic have been inaccessible to a huge number of pupils from marginalized and underprivileged backgrounds due to a lack of connectivity, devices, required skills, parental learning support, and access to technology resources. Only 13% of children and youth in South Asia had home Internet access in 2020 (UNICEF and ITU). The quality of students' Internet connections is often insufficient for online-based instruction, even in areas where students have some level of access to the Internet. In addition, not all students have benefited from distance learning that makes use of older technologies. Lessons broadcast on television or radio reached fewer than half of the intended recipients among primary school pupils in more than a third of low and lower-middl--income countries (UNICEF, 2020). The digital literacy of parents from low-income households is often insufficient for them to give their children the learning support they need when they engage in remote or online learning. Furthermore, online learning has not been able to accommodate students with impairments or special needs that require supplementary social and special education support (UNICEF, 2021a).

• **Inadequate Opportunities for Professional Growth**

Inadequate professional development is still a barrier to expanding the use of technology in the classroom, even when necessary resources are available. There is a lack of knowledge regarding how technology-integrated professional development might play out "on the ground", from the perspective of teachers (Wilkerson, Andrews, Shaban, Laina, & Gravel, 2016). There is no correlation between offering teachers professional development opportunities and increased levels of technology integration in the classroom, according to the available research. Teachers will incorporate technology into the curriculum to maximize its benefits on teaching and learning only if they are given the necessary knowledge, skills, resources, and support (Papanastasiou, Zemblyas, & Vrasidas, 2003).

• **Teachers' Lack of Proficiency in Modern Technologies and Educational Methods**

Regardless of a country's level of development, teachers' lack of digital competence is the most frequently cited obstacle to using technology effectively in the classroom (UNESCO, 2021). In particular, educators have lacked the necessary ICT and pedagogical competencies due to a lack of resources and opportunities. While nearly all teachers in Thailand and Singapore have some level of digital literacy, in countries like Kyrgyzstan, Malaysia, and the Philippines, that number drops below 5% (UNESCO, 2018).

• **Poor and Uneven Access to Information and Communication Technology**

The area is very unequally developed, with internet penetration ranging from over 90% in the most developed economies to about 15% in the least developing ones (ITU, 2021). There may also be an insufficient supply of electricity in these regions to facilitate the integration of ICT into the classroom (UNESCO, 2018). High-income countries and metropolitan centers tend to be where you find the greatest concentration of schools with adequate access to the Internet and computers (UNESCO & UNICEF, 2021a). There are also large gaps inside countries, which often mirror preexisting inequalities along such dimensions as socioeconomic standing, gender, and physical location. For instance, just 37% of individuals in rural areas have access to the Internet, as compared to 70.4% of people in metropolitan areas (ITU, 2021).

- **A Lack of Policy Direction for Digital Learning in Schools**

To promote and coordinate technological change activities across levels (national, sub-national, and local levels) and sectors, the government does not provide the essential policy direction. Public investment, legal and regulatory frameworks, and financial support must all be coordinated. UNESCO (2018) found that just 27% of countries with low or middle incomes in the area had a policy in place for digital distant learning.

3. DISCUSSION

Students' ability to tailor their learning experience to their specific needs is one of the benefits of technological advancement, which has been shown to increase both their learning and retention of course material (Machekhina, 2017). Bilyalova (2019) argues that the positive effects of technological change on schools outweigh the negative ones. Learning environments can be improved with the use of technology. In addition to having far-reaching effects on teaching and learning, it also gives students much more information than they would get from a traditional lecture style in the form of text, audio, and video. Bilyalova *et al.* (2020) argue that four distinct areas—hyper-collection of data, information resources, telecommunications, and management systems—can guide this new approach to teaching and learning for knowledge acquisition. Because "information technologies are new possibilities for new services and products, contributing towards acceleration in the pace of social, technical, cultural, and economic change", these approaches may be viewed as inconsistent and volatile despite the educational framework's intention to keep identifying possible necessities and opportunities in the development of new competencies within the educational population. Additionally, Al Rawashdeh *et al.* (2021), Gherhes *et al.* (2021), Muthuprasad *et al.* (2021), and Bilyalova *et al.* (2020) offered several of the most notable advantages and continuous benefits of e-learning instructions adopted and carried out effectively. They claim that the primary benefit is that students may participate actively and extensively in the pedagogy and feedback refinement process and that they can engage in self-directed learning experiences tailored to their requirements. Nevertheless, "information technologies are new possibilities for new services and products, contributing towards acceleration in the pace of social, technical, cultural, and economic change" (Field, 200), so the aforementioned methods can be seen as inconsistent and changeable, despite the educational framework's design to continuously keep identifying possible necessities and opportunities in the development of new competencies within the educational population. To keep up with the rapid pace of modern digitalization in terms of accessing and effectively delivering relevant information, both lecturers and students must continuously enhance and strengthen their application of information technologies to high standards (Bilyalova et al., 2020). Instead of being shackled by a teacher-centered approach, as was previously elaborated (Balluerka et al., 2008; Dervi & Becirovi, 2021), this would allow lecturers to take on the role of mentors to their students, guiding them through the learning process and inspiring them to become life-long learners.

4. IMPLICATIONS

The expansion and improvement of online learning rely heavily on state accreditation and regulations. Virtual educational businesses have sprung up all over the world because of the cost-savings afforded by the one-to-many and many-to-many models used in online schooling. There are both for-profit and non-profit businesses that offer classes specifically designed for the convenience of online learners. Governments often defend their role as gatekeepers in the educational system by arguing that schools are required to provide "public good". Education helps everyone in the community, not just the student who receives it. In contrast, a population with low levels of education harms the entire community. Governments have historically supported and regulated education due to its perceived social benefits and the widespread belief that citizens will remain in their home country after receiving a formal education. Online businesses threaten traditional methods of schooling because of their potential to expand and offer services at reduced prices. Although human capital in the form of a degree or certificate is invaluable, the cost of education, especially at the postsecondary level, can be prohibitive for some. Online education can be a cost-effective option for those seeking vocational or specialized education. Traditional educational institutions, which sometimes require substantial investments in tuition and time and cause students to carry enormous amounts of long-term debt, will face increased competition in the market for their services. Just like they do when choosing between current educational institutions, many students will compare the quality of credentials and quality of education against cost and debt commitments. Some established businesses may feel compelled to use digital technologies to lower prices or compete with newer businesses.

The availability and appeal of digital drift have an impact on the market for and the nature of instructional support. High fixed costs are a hallmark of conventional educational institutions, such as the wages of administrators and teachers. Since online schools avoid most of these costs, they can provide their services to students at much lower rates in exchange for less one-on-one time with their instructors. These businesses will entice people who otherwise will not be interested in or able to pursue higher education. Traditional educational institutions will also feel the effects of cost savings. If state governments see online education as a simple way to decrease expenses, they may encourage state-supported schools to replace costly traditional methods of education with less expensive online technology, increasing the current level of stress. The worldwide trend toward digital transformation in education is promising for the development of future-oriented, flexible education. It provides teachers with the adaptability and data-driven practices they need to meet the requirements of their students.

CONCLUSION

Education can benefit from the reasonable application of innovation and digital technology in today's hyper-connected environment. The benefits, of course, far outweigh the costs. However, since learning takes place in the classroom, teacher-student interaction will always be the key to classroom innovation. Despite its impressive persuasive potential, technology is ultimately just a tool, as man made it and not the other way around. However, technology is not meant to replace teachers. Another possibility is that the goal is to create a flexible learning environment that encourages growth. It shifts the focus of the classroom away from the traditional "sage on the stage" model and toward a more collaborative approach to education. Success in such endeavors will ultimately depend on how technology is used to keep students engaged. It might be frustrating and time-consuming, but a digital change in education can pave the way for novel connections, insights, and methods of instruction and collaboration. With the advent of new digital tools, educational initiatives are reaching more people than ever before. Teachers and students alike are benefiting from the increased opportunities presented by digital education, as they may now participate more actively in the teaching and learning process. Education has been revolutionized by the widespread availability of digital resources like cell phones, smart boards, tablets, laptops, and so on. One of the most cost-effective ways to teach pupils is becoming increasingly apparent: the Internet of Things (IoT). It is a robust framework that can be used to provide everyone with access to an exceptional education. EdTech firms are continually exploring new avenues for expanding student enrollment and participation in educational programs. Education in India's future will be shaped mostly by digital learning. The revolutionary impact that smart technologies are having on the educational system of our country as a whole is astounding. Rapid changes are occurring in the market for digital education in rural areas. Students in remote areas now have more access to online education because of cheaper, faster internet and direct-to-device technologies. There will soon be a plethora of EdTech startups in the market, offering a wide range of cutting-edge digital products to schools of all sizes. Traditional educational models will feel intense market pressure as digital ones gain traction, and governments that have historically funded education will feel pressure to reduce spending as a result. The lines between what we presently call education and other forms of social engagement involving the creation and dissemination of information will continue to blur. Again, this does not mean that we can no longer talk about education as a distinct field; rather, its borders will become more porous and its terminal points less certain. The social practices of learning in the digital age are a fusion of journalism, political commentary, and even the entertainment industry. As the boundaries between these fields continue to blur, the way education is practiced, financed, regulated, and accredited by governments, as well as the hiring and accreditation of teachers themselves, will all be affected.

REFERENCES

Al-Shakarchi, M. (2022). Digital Transformation in Education: The Complete Guide. Available from: https://www.d2l.com/en-eu/blog/digital-transformation-in-education-complete-guide/

Alliance for Affordable Internet, End Violence Against Children, Global Education Evidence Advisory Panel. (2022-2020). Meaningful Connectivity — unlocking the full power of internet access, COVID-19 and its implications for protecting children online, The Most Effective Ways to Keep Children Learning During and PostPandemic: Available from: https://a4ai.org/meaningful-connectivity/ Available from: https://www.endviolence.org/sites/default/files/paragraphs/download/COVID19%20and%20its%20implicatio ns%20for%20protecting%20children%20online_Final%20%28003%29_0.pdf Available from: https://thedocs.worldbank.org/en/doc/5f911bdf7c5c8abf060467865acf1abd0200022022/original/Prioritizing-Learning-GEEAP-Report-Final-01-24-2022.pdf

Clarifi Education PBC. (2023). 21 Benefits of Technology in Education. https://www.tryclarifi.com/benefits-of-technology-in-education/

Iivari, N., Molin-Juustila, T., Kinnula, M. (2016). The future digital innovators: Empowering the young generation with digital fabrication and making. *Proc. ICIS,* Dublin, Ireland1-8.

ITU, & UNESCO. (2021). The State of Broadband 2021: People-Centred Approaches for Universal Broadband. Available from: https://www.itu.int/dms_pub/itu-s/opb/pol/S-POL-BROADBAND.23--021-PDF-E.pdf

Kyriazi, T. (2015). Using technology to introduce frequent assessments for effective learning : Registering student perceptions. *Procedia Soc. Behav. Sci., 197*(February), 570-576. [http://dx.doi.org/10.1016/j.sbspro.2015.07.195]

Muneer, S. (2020). The Information System Management and Its Infrastructure for Supply Chain Management as Antecedents of Financial Performance. *Journal of Asian Finance, Economics and Business, 7*(1), 229-238.
[http://dx.doi.org/10.13106/jafeb.2020.vol7.no1.229]

Medina, M. (2023). Digital transformation challenges in education: 5 pitfalls to avoid. Available from: https://hospitalityinsights.ehl.edu/digital-transformation-challenges-education

McGregor, A.R. (2021). Advantages and Challenges of Digital Transformation in Education. Available from: https://www.projectcubicle.com/advantages-and-challenges-of-digital-transformation-in-the-education-sector/

Nguyen, X.T., Luu, Q.K. (2020). Factors Affecting Adoption of Industry 4.0 by Small- and Medium-Sized Enterprises: A Case in Ho Chi Minh City, Vietnam. *Journal of Asian Finance, Economics and Business, 7*(6), 255-264.
[http://dx.doi.org/10.13106/jafeb.2020.vol7.no6.255]

Omer, Oz. (2018). Academicians view on Digital Transformation in Education. Available from: https://www.researchgate.net/publication/333354818_Academicians'_views_on_digital_transfo

Papanastasiou, E.C., Zembylas, M., Vrasidas, C. (2003). Can computer use hurt science achievement? The USA results from PISA. *J. Sci. Educ. Technol., 12*(3), 325-332.

[http://dx.doi.org/10.1023/A:1025093225753]

Pokhrel, S., Chhetri, R. (2021). A Literature Review on Impact of COVID-19 Pandemic on Teaching and Learning. *Higher Education for the Future, 8*(1), 133-141.
[http://dx.doi.org/10.1177/2347631120983481]

Raja, R. (2018). Impact of modern technology in Education, Journal of Applied and Advanced research *Journal of Applied and Advanced Research, 3*(S1), 33-39.

Sharma, M. (2020). A Study on Digital Transformation and its Impact on Education Sector. *Palarch's Journal of Archaeology of Egypt/Egyptology, 17*(7), 16105-16108.

Shirshendu Roy. (2020). e-learning Scope and Trend in India Available from: https://www.researchgate.net/publication/338913710_elearning_Scope_and_Trend_in_India

Top 5 challenges facing education institutions in the age of digital transformation. Available from: https://www.osam.io/post/top-5-challenges-facing-education-institutions-in-the-age-of-digital-transformation

(2020). The Digital Transformation of Education: Connecting Schools, Empowering Learners. *Averting an Education Catastrophe for the World's Children.* Wiley Online Library.
[http://dx.doi.org/10.1002/9781119646495]

UNESCO, UNESCO & UNICEF. (2022-2021). Guidelines for ICT in education policies and masterplans, Rewired Global Declaration on Connectivity for Education, Japan Case Study: Situation Analysis on the Effects of and Responses to COVID-19 on the Education Sector in Asia. Available from: https://en.unesco.org/futuresofeducation/sites/default/files/2021-12/Rewired Global Declaration on Connectivity for Education.pdf

UNICEF. (2021). Practical Guide To Blended / Remote Learning and Children with Disabilities. Available from: https://www.unicef.org/media/100986/file/PRACTICAL%20GUIDE%20To%20blended.pdf a

UNICEF. (2021). How much does universal digital learning cost? Available from: https://www.un.org/sites/un2.un.org/files/sg_policy_brief_covid-19_and_education_august_2020.pdf b

United Nations. (2020-2019). Report of the Secretary-General Roadmap for Digital Cooperation, Right to education: the implementation of the right to education and Sustainable Development Goal 4 in the context of the growth of private actors in education - Report of the Special Rapporteur on the right to education. Available from: https://www.ohchr.org/en/documents/thematic-reports/ahrc4137-right-educat-on-implementation-right-education-and-sustainable b

Vial, G. (2019). Understanding digital transformation: A review and a research agenda. *The Journal of Strategic Information Systems., 28*(2), 118-144.
[http://dx.doi.org/10.1016/j.jsis.2019.01.003]

World Bank. (2021). Education Finance Watch. Available from: https://en.unesco.org/gem-report/educatio--finance-watch-2021

Wei, X., Saab, N., Admiraal, W. (2021). Assessment of cognitive, behavioral, and affective learning outcomes in massive open online courses: A systematic literature review. *Computers & Education, 163*, 104097.
[http://dx.doi.org/10.1016/j.compedu.2020.104097]

Wilkerson, M.H., Andrews, C., Shaban, Y., Laina, V., Gravel, B.E. (2016). What's the technology for? Teacher attention and pedagogical goals in a modeling-focused professional development workshop. *J. Sci. Teach. Educ., 27*(1), 11-33.
[http://dx.doi.org/10.1007/s10972-016-9453-8]

CHAPTER 3

Factors for Adopting Technology in the Education Sector

Abstract: Information communication and technology (ICT) is a key driver in most industries including education. The goal of this chapter is to look at the major factors that drive the adoption of digital tools in the education sector. Such factors include the role of educator/professor/lecturer, context factors, governmental actions, university factors, organizational culture and leadership, skills in information and communication technology, obtainability of resources, involved parties, value and developments, advances in technology, superiority of information, data science and business intelligence, and compatibility. Teachers and mentors should push their pupils to use ICT for research, communication, and problem-solving to boost their academic performance and opportunities. Both the availability of tools and the quality of those tools affect students' perspectives and intentions to engage in digital learning. ICT-based digital learning choices should be utilized by students. While some see ICT as a way to boost classroom efficiency, teamwork, the quality of instruction, and student outcomes, the reality is that its usage in schools has been widespread for only a short period and that many people are either uninterested or actively opposed to it.

Keywords: Adopting technology, Digital, Education sector, Factors, ICT.

1. INTRODUCTION

Many businesses are implementing extensive transformation programs to take advantage of the opportunities presented by the digital revolution or to simply keep up with the competition. Digital transformation in education talks about the widespread use of ICT to improve classroom instruction and student outcomes. When used effectively, technology can facilitate more equitable learning, provide access to knowledge and data, enhance the instructional process, and boost student achievement (UNESCO, 2021). In the wake of the COVID-19 pandemic, ICT has been increasingly acknowledged as a tool that may ensure students have access to a high-quality education even when institutions are closed. It can also be used to discover and implement novel approaches to education. In light of this growing interest, this chapter briefly investigates how the adoption of new digital tools in the classroom might aid in the revitalization of teaching and learning across all levels of schooling and improve the quality, efficiency, equity, and

Abdul-Mumin Khalid & Obeng Owusu-Boateng
All rights reserved-© 2024 Bentham Science Publishers

sustainability of the educational system as a whole. Very few studies have examined the transformative potential of ICT in schools; instead, they focused on the needs and impediments to adoption. Therefore, it is vital to think of the adoption of technology as a decision made by the teacher based on a positive set of attitudes and beliefs that influence the attitude-intention-behavior relationship if one is to gain an understanding of the process. The determinants of this adoption include social influence and conducive settings, as well as the expectation of performance and effort, among others (Aleksandrov et al., 2018). Action research, or reflecting on and refining learning tasks and activities that incorporate digital tools for pedagogical purposes, is one such circumstance. The teacher's characteristics, such as gender, age, experience, and willingness to volunteer, also matter. Finally, the deployment of technology is not enough to alter education on its own; teachers also need to be retrained to create a more innovative, collaborative, individualized, and supportive classroom setting. The term "digital transformation" refers to the process of permeating an organization with digital technology to make major changes to its operations and increase its value to students. As a result of this shift in mindset, businesses must be willing to constantly question established practices, try new things, and learn from their mistakes. Digital transformation is at the top of the company's list of tasks, yet many academic institutions are inaccurate in their assessments of their levels of digital transformation.

The need for digital literacy and digital equity is the driving force behind most of the important self-learning and ICT trends, especially in developing nations. Internal circumstances, such as the need for professional development, discipline, systematicity, and creative-reflective thinking, are necessary for educators to realize the relevance of digital self-learning in enhancing their professional competence. Similarly, research shows that social networks have a significant role in empowering educators to use ICT. The widespread adoption of m-learning (using mobile devices like smartphones, tablets, laptops, and netbooks) in higher education institutions has the potential to expand access to higher education, but it will only succeed with the help of automation of services and the digital savviness of faculty members. Therefore, it is necessary to examine and analyze essential elements responsible for adopting technology to improve student achievements in terms of ICT use and digital learning technologies. In light of this, the authors of this research set out to determine what factors affect students' adoption of ICT and digital learning technologies at the tertiary level. As a result, progress toward the objectives is slow, and much work remains. In this paper, we will examine the most important factors for moving forward and completing a successful digital transformation in the arena of electronic education.

1.1. Contributions of the Chapters

The findings of this study add to the body of knowledge in management, both theoretically and practically. Governments can use the findings of the evaluation to inform their decisions about higher education. It is useful for private schools, colleges, and universities that are aggressively trying to expand their enrollment through digital means. Understanding what motivates today's learners to adopt or not accept specific services in online learning is now crucial. These are vital questions, and the present study provides answers that could aid educational institutions in formulating effective methods in response to them. Therefore, schools should think carefully about everything when formulating rules to draw in and keep online students.

2. LITERATURE

2.1. Digital Transformation

No industry, no matter how big or narrow its focus is, can afford to ignore the digital transformation (DT). By adopting an entirely novel leadership mode, innovative instruments, new techniques of work, and new perspectives and businesses, this strategy enables management systems to improve their processes, resulting in improved performance, effectiveness, and competitiveness. DT is now an important strategic issue for any executive to address. It expands students' horizons outside the classroom by providing means to speed up their development while also generating long-term competitive benefits and ensuring the safety of their operations. By streamlining administrative procedures and student-teacher communication, DT boosts the educational system's bottom line. The term "digital transformation" refers to the process through which a company modifies its basic operations to better serve its customers. Customers in the academic sector may include students, teachers, and administrators, among others. The educational sector is becoming increasingly competitive, making digital transformation a must for educators to adapt and thrive in the new digital world by embracing digital technologies, approaches, and mindsets. A thorough and long-lasting digital transformation requires an understanding of the obstacles that may stand in the way. This paper aims to survey the literature on incorporating digital transformation into management education and to examine its practical application concerning four dimensions: time, place of origin, industry, and the focus of digital transformation.

2.2. Digital Transformation in Education

Technology has an impact on every part of our educational system, from K-12 to higher learning. The transmission and reception of information are undergoing radical changes as a result of the rapid development of technology. The proliferation of digital technologies has paved the way for cutting-edge forms of communication, speeding up the dissemination of knowledge in academic institutions. It is changing how we think about teaching and learning altogether. The use of digital technology to alter education is a once-in-a-generation chance to rethink teaching and learning in light of their far-reaching effects on the economy, society, and industry. The complete spectrum of HEI operations is relevant to the study of the digital transformation of higher education, which is a vast and complicated field of inquiry. According to Brown, Reinitz, and Wetze (2020), digital transformation is "a series of deep and coordinated culture, workforce, and technology shifts that enable new educational and operating models and transform an institution's business model, strategic directions, and value." The term "digital transformation" is often used to refer to developments in many different areas, including computing, society, creativity, and even project management. There is more to digital transformation than just using new tools (Sarnok *et al.*, 2020). The impact of digital transformation on higher education institutions extends far beyond the realm of information technology. All digital initiatives in higher education must be tied to the institution's overarching mission and goals (Sarnok *et al.*, 2019). The shift to a digital economy relies on the educational system undergoing a digital makeover. Building an infrastructure that actively introduces innovative technologies, provides management system flexibility, introduces cutting-edge educational technologies, and constructs individualized models of learning is integral to the process. The rise of digital technology is impacting both virtual and physical classrooms. Faster and more efficient online learning is emerging as a result of the proliferation of digital technologies for education (Mundy *et al.*, 2012). The usage of machine learning and AI is on the rise; more sophisticated learning management systems (LMSs) are being developed, *etc.* The shift from classroom instruction to online education is indicative of the transformations occurring in traditional classroom settings. Learning institutions are not required, and students are free to pursue their education anywhere they like. Online courses also have phantom educators and an entirely computerized testing and certification process.

2.3. Factors

Digital transformation is still more of an evolution than a revolution, and a successful transition implements the best solutions for the current state of the business methodically. The key practical factors of digitization are the foundation on which digital transformation is built.

2.4. The Educator, Professor, or Lecturer

The teacher is often cited as one of the influential variables in students' success when using technology in the classroom. Teachers' attitudes toward and comfort with technologies have been identified as a crucial element in the use of such tools in the classroom (Mustapha *et al.*, 2019). A teacher is not required to have a positive attitude about technology or to incorporate it into their lessons if they do not wish to. Proper usage of technology in education also appears to be influenced by teachers' own instructional mindsets and pedagogical philosophies. Deployment of technological advances may be affected by factors such as an individual's degree of schooling, age, gender, level of technological expertise, degree of comfort using computers in the classroom, and general attitude toward such devices (Mustapha, 2016). Teachers are urged to accept and incorporate ICT into lessons, but the technology's efficacy is determined not by its presence but by teachers' readiness to use it (Mundy *et al.*, 2012). The willingness of educators to adopt and implement technological tools in the classroom is crucial. Anxiety, lack of confidence and competence, and fear are often the reasons why information and communication technology (ICT) is put on the back burner in favor of more traditional forms of education (Russell & Bradley, 1997). Therefore, it is important to comprehend the factors that shape the likelihood of teachers adopting and using ICT in their lessons. The tutor's responsibilities have expanded beyond simply imparting knowledge to a class. The role of the instructor has changed as the online education sector has developed. If a student has faith in the quality of their instructor, that person can act as a peacemaker, guide, and problem solver for both software and hardware issues. A good instructor will inspire their students to try out new e-learning environments and confidently use their newfound digital knowledge. Group instructional help, holding in-person or online classes for specialized assistance, emailing and constructing online groups, and providing electronic feedback for online assignments are all examples of how the role of the tutor has expanded over time (Kear *et al.*, 2014; Teo & Luan, 2011).

2.5. Factors in Context

Government policy decisions, institutional tactics, and the actions of key actors, such as students and faculty in higher education, are all affected by the context in which they are made. A digital education ecosystem, which may include private sector enterprises, non-governmental organizations, and other agencies having a role in digital learning, is one of these elements (Brown *et al.*, 2020). Other aspects include the state of the economy, the population's attitudes and values, and the history and development of technology.

2.6. Governmental Actions

The public policies that are in place can either facilitate or inhibit the digitization of universities. Some of these policies, including those concerning the nation's infrastructure, do not pertain to institutions of higher learning. The full range of policy levers available to governments is being used to advance digitalization in higher education, including the development of national targets, strategies, and bodies to facilitate this shift, as well as the regulation (for example, regarding the quality or data protection), funding, and the dissemination of information to all stakeholders about the opportunities afforded by a digitalized higher education system (OECD, 2021). Higher education institutions (HEIs) can greatly benefit from public policies that provide incentives and assistance for expanding and improving their digital practices. Meanwhile, institutional methods play a major role in either encouraging or discouraging the use of technology in classrooms and other learning environments (Brown *et al.*, 2020).

2.7. University Factors

An educational institution's goal is not to solve any one problem so much as to alleviate the strain brought on by demands that are beyond or supersede the normative sphere of authority. They also vehemently resist any changes that would place constraints on the status quo. What seems like an obvious benefit to an outsider may be deeply unpleasant to an internal stakeholder group if it requires the business to alter its values and procedures (Mustapha *et al.*, 2019). As new technologies emerge, it will be necessary to make significant adjustments to how classes are taught, how much money is spent, and even how the institution is structured as a whole. More specifically, it is assumed that companies have a structure that prevents extensive use of computers because of their fundamental aversion to change. The qualities that teachers already possess are enhanced by institutional variables. There is a strong correlation between the amount of time teachers spend teaching and their level of training in the use of technology. They argue that school administrators and trainers have a responsibility to "provide extensive training on educational technology, but should also facilitate a contribution to teaching improvement" (p. 262). Access to technology was also highlighted by Mustapha (2016). As a result, it is important to get an appreciation for the institutional factors that shape educators' decisions to adopt and implement ICT in the classroom.

2.8. Organizational Culture and Leadership

Successful digital transformation requires leadership and a culture similar to that of a winning team, where individuals are encouraged and supported to contribute to their full potential (Abbas, 2022). School technology leadership is a more significant predictor of teachers' use of computers in instruction than is infrastructural support (Anderson & Dexter, 2005). According to Yee (2000), instructors are more likely to incorporate technology into their courses when their leader has a clear plan for its use and communicates that plan to them.

2.9. Skills in Information and Communication Technology

According to the definition provided by van Braak *et al.* (2004), computer competence refers to the ability to use a wide variety of software programs for a variety of tasks. Expertise in using computers is a strong indicator of whether or not teachers would use ICT in the classroom. There is evidence to suggest that most educators who have a negative or neutral outlook on the use of ICT in the classroom lack the knowledge and skills necessary to make an "informed decision" (Bordbar, 2010). Peralta and Costa (2007) conducted qualitative multiple case-study studies in five European nations to examine primary school teachers' competence and confidence level in using ICT in teaching practice; they discovered that technical competence influenced Italian teachers' use of ICT in the classroom. However, if educational interventions are to be effective and efficient, teachers stress the importance of pedagogical and didactic competencies. In Portugal, educators expressed divergent opinions on which skills are most crucial for using ICT in the classroom. Students-turned-teachers highlighted technical competence and pedagogical efficiency as crucial to integrating ICT in teaching and learning processes, while seasoned educators emphasized the importance of a positive mindset toward technology in the classroom.

3. OBTAINABILITY OF RESOURCES

The availability of resources refers to the accessibility of digital study materials. According to Singh (2016), all digital materials, whether online or offline, used by college students are considered technological resources. eBooks and other electronic books, as well as online journals, articles, blogs, and other forms of free educational content, are available to students today. Learners are influenced to embrace e-learning tools when they have access to the materials they need (Salloum *et al.*, 2019).

3.1. Involved Parties, Value, and Developments

Focusing on the most important procedures for the company's performance requires an in-depth knowledge of the digital trends in the sector and the cooperation of partners and suppliers that are best in class (Abbas, 2022).

3.2. Advances in Technology

The ability to adapt and fully leverage the cutting-edge technology available now is crucial to achieving a successful digital transformation (Abbas, 2022). The digital infrastructure of the institution, according to Kuzu (2020) and Navaridas-Nalda *et al.* (2020), is crucial to the success of digital transformation. Increasing contact between professors and students on university-invested technological platforms or social networks and providing students with support in accessing digital resources are key to the rapid success of the university's digital transformation process. Students' optimistic views of digital transformation and their readiness to implement it soon are shaped by its interaction, low cost, and perceived utility, according to Singh *et al.* (2020). Teachers' adoption of technological tools is influenced by several factors, not the least of which is the technology itself. There are currently competing theories on how best to incorporate technology's potentially transformative benefits into the classroom (Mustapha, 2016). This leads educators to question the morality of using technology in the classroom. As technology evolves, it becomes increasingly difficult for educators to keep up. This is because new technological hardware and software are released regularly, making it difficult and intimidating for educators to keep up. Teachers have limited contact time with their students and cannot afford to waste it troubleshooting technological issues they may or may not be able to resolve. This makes the use of technology less appealing to most educators. Therefore, teachers may choose not to incorporate technology into their lessons if there is not a clear necessity for doing so and enough assistance is not available (Mustapha, 2018).

3.3. Superiority of Information

The quality of the data and other content delivered by computer networks is known as "informational quality." According to Gustavsson and Wanstrom (2009), "the ability to satisfy the learners' informational needs" is the definition of information quality. Interest in using online learning platforms is boosted when the information they provide is clear, straightforward, and trustworthy. There is a favorable correlation between the quality of the information provided and the likelihood that a learner may use technological aids (Sharma *et al.*, 2016; Tarhini *et al.*, 2016, 2017; Panigrahi *et al.*, 2020). When students are presented with confusing or unreliable content while employing technology-based methods of instruction, however, their motivation to adopt these strategies decreases.

3.4. Data Science and Business Intelligence

Using the data generated by automation and digitization to inform and guide decisions is the next step in an iterative process of continuous improvement (Abbas, 2022).

3.5. Compatibility

Compatibility refers to how well students feel that they can use their existing values, beliefs, and information behaviors when using technology to study for a course. When it comes to adopting new technologies, compatibility is defined as "the degree to which a new technology is continuously seen with prior experience, existing values, and the needs of latent adopters" (Rogers, 2003). It was also shown that a student's intention to adopt learning technologies was substantially correlated with the degree to which those technologies were compatible with the student's existing knowledge and skills.

4. IMPLICATIONS

Users' perceptions of the technology's worth may vary according to their individual preferences and needs, alongside the technology's specifics. The findings of this study have the potential to enhance the suggested project for colleges and other educational institutions by providing contemporary relevance for teaching and learning practice. It is imperative to define the goals of digital transformation and rally the troops (including investors) behind the new plan of attack. If you want to succeed in your digital transformation efforts, setting measurable KPIs is a must. It is important to reevaluate both front- and back-end systems to ensure a consistent, unified, and natural interaction for learners and, ultimately, staff. Embrace modern tools to build credibility and keep up with rising student demands. Make sure your information and messages can be delivered across different platforms without being disrupted by algorithm updates. Students' effective use of technology in the classroom depends on teachers' and administrators' familiarity with and ability to work around the challenges inherent in such an endeavor. The simple addition of technology to classrooms and schools is not the answer to the problem of low academic performance. The district needs to perform long-term research to determine if the tools being utilized are beneficial before it can develop a strategy to aid schools in overcoming these internal and external barriers. By introducing ICT into pedagogy, teachers can help students develop positive feelings about technology and increase their interest in using it for digital learning. Teachers and mentors should push their pupils to use ICT for research, communication, and problem-solving to boost their academic performance and opportunities. Both the availability of tools and the quality of those tools affect students' perspectives on and intentions to engage in digital learning. ICT-based digital learning choices should be utilized by students.

CONCLUSION

Education has been profoundly affected by the digital revolution. The potential of digital technologies to enhance education has piqued the attention of many in the academic world. In recent years, it has been challenging to provide education *via* a variety of learning modalities. Technology has allowed us to overcome many of the barriers to effective teamwork, commerce, information access, and communication. The ability to effectively use digital information is crucial for modern citizenship and professional success. The ability to continue learning indefinitely is seen as a key benefit of widespread access to digital knowledge, and digital literacy is seen as the basis for this capability. Educators have a crucial role in fostering digital literacy among the population. As a result, universities should reconsider how they might best put digital information technology to work in the classroom. There are a few problems with the current study. Many professionals and students now use ICT daily. Literacy in the use of technology guarantees that resources can be put to good use, paving the way for a country's progress. The traditional educational system will get a boost from the incorporation of ICT, broadening the horizons of both students and educators. The evidence in this chapter demonstrates that the reasons for this are more nuanced than what meets the eye, and an interactive model constructed for this chapter was able to tease them out. While some see ICT as a way to boost classroom efficiency, teamwork, the quality of instruction, and student outcomes, the reality is that its usage in schools has been widespread for only a short period and that many people are either uninterested or actively opposed to it.

RECOMMENDATIONS

Because the study indicated that the high cost of funding ICT activities is negatively influencing ICT integration, it is also recommended that the government enhance the ICT budget to solve adoption difficulties in secondary schools. Budgetary support for information and communication technologies (ICT) should be increased to strengthen the work of the Ministry of Information and Communication and the Ministry of Education to lower the overall cost of adopting ICT. The study found that unfavorable user attitudes slow down the full realization of ICT potential and that IT literacy levels are extremely low in secondary schools. As a result, the study suggests that the government, through its ministries, agencies, and other stakeholders, do more to improve the ICT infrastructure in schools, particularly regarding educational support software, ICT interconnectivity, internet connection speed, and policy guidelines regarding ICT work. This will ensure that the slow rate of ICT adoption is reversed and the rate of diffusion in schools is increased by addressing both the psychological and technical skill preparation of teachers.

REFERENCES

Abbas, M. (2022). The 5 Success Factors for Digital Transformation: Digital Transformation in the Waste and Recycling Industries. Available from: https://www.amcsgroup.com/blogs/the-5-success-factors-for-digital-transformation/#the-five-success-factors-for-digital-transformation

Anderson, R.E., Dexter, S. (2005). School technology leadership: An empirical investigation of prevalence and effect. *Educ. Adm. Q., 41*(1), 49-82.
[http://dx.doi.org/10.1177/0013161X04269517]

Aleksandrov, A. A., Kapyrin, P. A., Meshkov, N.A., Popovich, A.E., Proletarsky, A.V. (2018). Gamification in the advanced higher professional education: Fundamentals of theory and experience of use *International Journal of Civil Engineering and Technology, 9*(11), 1800-1808.

Brown, M., Reinitz, B., Wetzel, K. (2020). Digital Transformation Signals: Is Your Institution on the Journey? Available from: https://er.educause.edu/blogs/2019/10/digital-transformation-signals-is--our-institution-on-the-journey (Accessed on: 26 November 2020).

Gustavsson, M., Wänström, C. (2009). Assessing information quality in manufacturing planning and control processes. *Int. J. Qual. Reliab. Manage., 26*(4), 325-340.
[http://dx.doi.org/10.1108/02656710910950333]

Kear, K., Donelan, H., Williams, J. (2014). Using wikis for online group projects: Student and tutor perspectives. *Int. Rev. Res. Open Distance Learn., 15*(4), 70-90.
[http://dx.doi.org/10.19173/irrodl.v15i4.1753]

Kuzu, Ö. H. (2020). Digital transformation in higher education: A case study on strategic plans. *Vysshee Obrazovanie v Rossii (Higher Education in Russia), 29*(3), 9-23.
[http://dx.doi.org/10.1177/2158244012440813]

Mustapha, A. (2018). The importance of Technology in Teaching and learning.*Teaching with Technology: Perspectives, Challenges and Future Challenges..* New York: Nova Science Publishers.

Mustapha, A. (2016). Effects of simulation on the achievement, retention and skill performance of motor vehicle mechanic in Niger State technical colleges [unpublished med thesis]. *Thesis: Minna: National Open University of Nigeria.*

Mustapha, A. (2019). *Factors Affecting the Utilization and Adoption of Technology in Education.* IntechOpen.

Mundy, M.A., Kupczynski, L., Kee, R. (2012). Teacher's perception of technology use in school. *SAGE Open, 2*(1)
[http://dx.doi.org/10.1177/2158244012440813]

Navaridas-Nalda, F., Clavel-San Emeterio, M., Fernández-Ortiz, R., Arias-Oliva, M. (2020). The strategic influence of school principal leadership in the digital transformation of schools. *Comput. Human Behav., 112*, 106481.
[http://dx.doi.org/10.1016/j.chb.2020.106481]

OECD. (2021). *OECD Economic Surveys: Hungary..* Paris: OECD Publishing.

OECD. (2020). A Roadmap Toward a Common Framework for Measuring the Digital Economy: Report for the G20 Digital Economy Task Force Available from: https://www.oecd.org/digital/ieconomy/roadmap-toward-a-common-framework-for-measuring-the-digital-economy.pdf

OECD. (2020). *Resourcing Higher Education: Challenges, Choices and Consequences.* Paris: Higher Education, OECD Publishing.

[http://dx.doi.org/10.1787/735e1f44-en]

OECD. (2019). *Benchmarking Higher Education System Performance*. Paris: Higher Education, OECD Publishing.
[http://dx.doi.org/10.1787/be5514d7-en]

OECD. (2019). *Going Digital: Shaping Policies, Improving Lives.*. Paris: OECD Publishing.

Panigrahi, R., Srivastava, P.R., Panigrahi, P.K. (2020). Effectiveness of e-learning: the mediating role of student engagement on perceived learning effectiveness. *Inf. Technol. People, 34*(7), 1840-1862.
[http://dx.doi.org/10.1108/ITP-07-2019-0380]

Rogers, E.M. (2003). *Diffusion of Innovations*. (5th ed.). New York, NY: The Free Press.

Sarnok, K., Wannapiroo, P., Nilsook, P. (2019). Digital Learning Ecosystem by Using Digital Storytelling for Teacher Profession Students. *Int. J. Inf. Educ. Technol., 9*(1), 21-26.
[http://dx.doi.org/10.18178/ijiet.2019.9.1.1167]

Sarnok, K., Wannapiroon, P., Nilsook, P. (2020). Dtl-eco system by digital storytelling to develop knowledge and digital intelligence for teacher profession students. *Int. J. Inf. Educ. Technol., 10*(12), 865-872.
[http://dx.doi.org/10.18178/ijiet.2020.10.12.1472]

Singh, A., Sharma, S., Paliwal, M. (2021). Adoption intention and effectiveness of digital collaboration platforms for online learning: the Indian students' perspective. *Interact. Technol. Smart Educ., 18*(4), 493-514.
[http://dx.doi.org/10.1108/ITSE-05-2020-0070]

Salloum, S.A., Al-Emran, M., Shaalan, K., Tarhini, A. (2019). Factors affecting the E-learning acceptance: A case study from UAE. *Educ. Inf. Technol., 24*(1), 509-530.
[http://dx.doi.org/10.1007/s10639-018-9786-3]

Sharma, S.K., Al-Badi, A.H., Govindaluri, S.M., Al-Kharusi, M.H. (2016). Predicting motivators of cloud computing adoption: A developing country perspective. *Comput. Human Behav., 62*, 61-69.
[http://dx.doi.org/10.1016/j.chb.2016.03.073]

Singh, J. (2016). Acceptance of technology-enhanced learning: a study among technical students in India *Thesis: Indian Institute of Management, Indore.*

Tarhini, A., Hone, K., Liu, X., Tarhini, T. (2016). Examining the moderating effect of individual level cultural values on users' acceptance of e-learning in developing countries: a structural equation modeling of an extended technology acceptance model. *Interact. Learn. Environ., 25*(3), 1-23.
[http://dx.doi.org/10.1080/10494820.2015.1122635]

Tarhini, A., Masa'deh, R., Al-Busaidi, K.A., Mohammed, A.B., Maqableh, M. (2017). Factors influencing students' adoption of e-learning: a structural equation modeling approach. *Journal of International Education in Business, 10*(2), 164-182.
[http://dx.doi.org/10.1108/JIEB-09-2016-0032]

Teo, T., Luan, W.S., Thammetar, T., Chattiwat, W. (2011). Assessing e-learning acceptance by university students in Thailand. *Australas. J. Educ. Technol., 27*(8), 27.
[http://dx.doi.org/10.14742/ajet.898]

Tungpantong, C., Nilsook, P., Wannapiroon, P. (2021). A Conceptual Framework of Factors for Information Systems Success to Digital Transformation in Higher Education Institutions. *9th International Conference on Information and Education Technology, ICIET,* Okayama, Japan57-62.
[http://dx.doi.org/10.1109/ICIET51873.2021.9419596]

UNESCO. (2021). Rewired Global Declaration on Connectivity for Education. Available from: https://en.unesco.org/futuresofeducation/sites/default/files/2021-12/Rewired Global Declaration on Connectivity for Education.pdf.

Yee, D. (2000). Images of school principals' information and communications technology leadership. *Technol. Pedagogy Educ., 9*(3), 287-302.
[http://dx.doi.org/10.1080/14759390000200099]

CHAPTER 4

The Adoption of E-Learning in the Education Sector

Abstract: Technology has recently become a major component of the educational field and learning process as it provides students with opportunities to learn more effectively and operate efficiently in this age of technological advances. The study has identified the factors among students that can enable or inhibit students from using online learning platforms. Based on the theoretical foundation, the factors influencing e-learning are environmental, organizational, technological (smart-device use), subjective norms, self-efficacy, accessibility and flexibility. User adoption of e-learning is greatly influenced by the strength and dependability of the underlying information technology infrastructure. The present state of e-learning in universities and the results of previous studies on the topic are also described.

Keywords: Adoption, Education, e-Learning, Online, Platform, Technology.

1. INTRODUCTION

All facets of daily life have been altered by the proliferation of ICT due to the constant improvement of technology applications and tools (Kjellsdotter, 2020).

The internet has made the world a smaller place, eliminating physical barriers to what were once considered professional and personal relationships across the globe (Memon & Meyer, 2017). Similarly, ICT has created a new trend in the educational system that has brought about considerable improvements with good effects. The use of information and communication technology (ICT) tools in the classroom has many advantages that add up to a more thorough and effective grasp of difficult-to-grasp scientific principles and methods.

Technology in higher education is changing the way professors do their jobs, particularly in terms of the services they provide to students (Al-Ghurbani *et al.*, 2022). Professors work to increase the amount of technology available to students as colleges and universities increase their use of technology in instruction (Al-Ghurbani *et al.*, 2022). Insight, investigation, and communication across national boundaries have all been revolutionized by technological advancements. Due to technological advancements, it is now possible for universities to teach anyone,

Abdul-Mumin Khalid & Obeng Owusu-Boateng
All rights reserved-© 2024 Bentham Science Publishers

anywhere in the world. More and more schools are seeing the benefits of incorporating technology into the classroom. This rapid pace of period integration has provided higher education with a model to explore innovative methods of instruction. The goals of Al-Awidi and Aldhafeeri (2017), Tarman (2016, 2017), and Tarman and Chigisheva (2017)—proponents of digitizing the curriculum in higher education—are to raise standards of instruction and to broaden and update their application. The shift from conventional methods of education to those that make use of modern information and communication technology is well underway at present. The Faculty of Distance Learning places a strong emphasis on the organization of the learning process in an online learning environment, and this area of academic study is constantly developing and expanding. The term "e-learning" can also apply to the use of ICTs to improve students' access to online teaching and learning materials, as well as to the provision of Web 2.0-based collaboration environments and tools for students. Web 2.0 is a collection of programs that enhance and modify social interaction and communication (Martins et al., 2019). The term "e-learning" is broad enough to encompass numerous contexts, procedures, and instructional strategies. This research synthesis looks at the effects of information and communication technology (ICT) on college and university students. It is clear from the conclusions of the topics investigated under e-learning literature that some areas, such as comprehensive aspects leading to e-learning, still require continuing investigation. Most studies only looked at one stakeholder, like students, revealing a large gap in the research. The goal of this chapter is to investigate the causes behind the expansion of e-learning and to present methods for attracting more interested parties.

Not many of the publications we looked at employed the TOE framework (Namisiko, Munialo, & Nyongesa, 2014). To our knowledge, the TOE paradigm is the only one to consider all three of these important aspects of technology adoption (Nkhoma & Dang, 2013). When studying the adoption of technological innovation like e-learning, the TOE framework considers the institution's technological, environmental, and organizational aspects from a broad perspective. None of the competing hypotheses adequately accounted for the interplay between the technological, environmental, and organizational factors of adoption. Therefore, this chapter blends TAM with TEO conceptually to comprehend such elements that influence e-learning.

1.1. Contribution

This research will help universities understand the barriers to e-learning and work toward resolving them. This will allow universities to focus their efforts and resources where they will have the greatest impact, increasing the likelihood of the program's success. If it works, it will allow universities to begin using e-learning, which will provide a new medium for efficient education and wider participation. The research has practical implications since it alerts university administration to the existence of certain characteristics that promote or inhibit the adoption of e-learning. Universities taking the plunge into e-learning adoption now have access to information that was probably previously unavailable to universities in developing countries: a thorough understanding of the nature and determinants of e-learning's success. Therefore, colleges and universities considering implementing an e-learning program should evaluate their IT infrastructure, perceived user-friendliness, course material, and e-learning curriculum with a critical eye. Those involved in creating and implementing e-learning systems, as well as academic instructors and administrators, will find this chapter useful. This chapter fills a need in the literature by addressing the dearth of studies focusing on e-learning in less-developed nations.

2. LITERATURE

2.1. E-Learning

Studies that made use of technology or electronic appliances in any way, shape, or form are included here. In higher education, "e-learning" is defined as "the application of ICT to improve or facilitate studying" (OECD, 2005).

Hsbollah and Idris (2009) describe a learning care management system as a web-based educational system that makes use of information technology and networked computers. E-learning, or electronic learning, has emerged as a result of developments in information and communication technology.

E-learning is the teaching-learning process that takes place in an electronic environment, also known as virtual instruction, *via* the Internet, online learning, and distance learning (Singh & Thurman, 2019). With the advent of e-learning, traditional obstacles to the dissemination of information have been overcome.

Therefore, it has become a versatile and inexpensive method of giving high-quality education to those who would otherwise have little or no opportunity to receive it. Traditional education relies heavily on e-learning (Massive open online courses (MOOCs)) because of its adaptability, wide resource-sharing capacity, and cost-effective scalability (Allen & Seaman, 2011). Learning and technology are two distinct aspects of e-learning (Aparicio *et al.*, 2016). Aparico *et al.* (2016) define learning as "the cognitive process of acquiring knowledge and new skills", with technology acting as a "powerful enabler" of this process. Computer-assisted instruction (CAI; Zinn, 2003) is the foundation of today's most popular online education platforms. People, technology, and services are the three pillars upon which the theoretical framework for creating an e-learning system rests (Aparicio *et al.*, 2016). E-learning technologies allow for direct or indirect contact with many groups of individuals and users, which is essential for any successfully implemented e-learning system (Aparicio *et al.*, 2016). The focus of the technology component is to furnish the necessary technical backing for content integration, communication, and the accessibility of collaborative tools (Aparicio *et al.*, 2016). E-learning services and activities are developed to complement e-learning pedagogical and instructional modalities and tactics (Aparicio *et al.*, 2016) as part of an e-learning system's service component.

2.2 Factors for Adopting E-Learning

2.2.1. Subjective Norm

When people talk about what they "should" or "should not" do, they are referring to subjective norms (Fishbein & Ajzen, 1975). According to Taylor and Todd (1995), "subjective norms" are an individual's impressions of the social pressures to engage in the behavior in the issue. Direct and indirect effects of subjective norms on the intention to utilize information technology have been proven to be substantial (Venkatesh & Davis, 2000). Nevertheless, research findings tend to be contradictory. The impacts of subjective norms appear to fade gradually and only stay relevant in required situations, according to some research (Venkatesh & Davis, 2000), while other research has found the opposite to be true. Recently, Lee (2006) discovered that individual norms had a considerable impact on how helpful people thought something was.

2.2.2. Culture

One must consider one's own learning culture and approach. The adoption of any e-learning system is complicated by variances in learning styles and cultural backgrounds among its users. The learning preferences and styles of students, as well as their e-learning environment, should be taken into account while designing and developing an e-learning system (Irfan *et al.*, 2020; Islam *et al.*, 2015). To ensure the greatest possible results from e-learning systems, it is important to take into account students' learning styles (Islam *et al.*, 2015; Zalat *et al.*, 2021).

2.2.3. The Interaction of Systems

Student-to-student contacts, faculty-to-student interactions, and the resulting student-to-student collaboration in learning are the cornerstones of the educational experience. Innovations in e-learning have been driven mostly by tools that facilitate more active participation on the part of students. Synchronous or asynchronous communication is possible. One aspect that may influence students' willingness to accept e-learning systems is, thus, the degree of system engagement available to them. According to Davis, Bagozzi, and Warshaw (1989), the perceived usefulness and ease of use of a system are directly related to its objective features. Davis (1989) discovered this in his research on the diffusion of e-mail and text editors; he showed that the TAM fully mediates the impact of system attributes on usage behavior.

2.2.4. Unique to Each Educational Institution

Technologists believe that the company's existing technology stack, as well as the perceived relative benefit, compatibility difficulty, trialability, and observability of the application, all play a role in its rate of adoption.

Businesses with greater levels of technological competency are more likely to implement e-commerce since the success of IT adoption is determined by the relevance of internal technology resources (infrastructure, technical skills, developers, and user time).

Organizational assistance is any action taken, formal or informal, to help staff members learn and use a new system. Providing the requisite infrastructure, setting up specialized helpdesks, employing system and business process experts, and sending employees to off-the-clock training are all examples of how businesses may lend a hand (Venkatesh and Bala, 2008). According to their findings, organizational backing can be a major factor in how practical and simple users find something to be perceptions of external control, which can be attributed in large part to organizational backing.

Additionally, organizational assistance, especially in the context of complex systems, can alleviate worries related to their utilization. Before a full-scale rollout of e-learning can occur, it is necessary to train staff and students and make a choice about beta testing (Tucker and Gentry, 2009). There is also a significant time commitment involved in creating and updating e-learning content (Eke, 2010). This is because reengineering the course for online distribution can often require significant time and effort on the part of the teachers. Managers (*e.g.*, direct supervisors, middle managers, and senior executives) are important sources of interventions, according to Jasperson *et al.* (2005), cited by Venkatesh and Bala (2008). Managers can intervene either indirectly (*e.g.*, by sponsoring or championing, providing resources, and issuing directives and/or mandates) or directly (*e.g.*, by using features of IT, directing modification or enhancement of IT applications, incentive structures, or work). Nanayakkara (2007) observed that staff adoption of e-learning was influenced by organizational factors, including faculty facilitation of staff skill development in e-content design and delivery and staff release time for online engagement. Help-desk services to complement e-delivery, training in information and communication technology to facilitate effective communication and e-learning-specific skills can all considerably increase employee interest in and uptake of e-learning.

2.2.5. Convenience

Because of the flexibility they provide, e-learning technologies are preferable to traditional classroom settings. Tsuma (2021) reports that students can review previously delivered lectures without negatively impacting the comprehension of their classmates. Forums and communities centered on massive open online courses increase the utility of these e-learning resources (Tsuma, 2021).

2.2.6. Self-Efficacy

In the field of social learning theory, self-efficacy is a key notion (Bandura, 1977). One's confidence in one's abilities to carry out specific behaviors or complete specific tasks is an example of self-efficacy. Multiple studies have shown that an individual's confidence in his or her ability to succeed at a task has a significant impact on his or her choice of tasks, the length of time spent attempting those tasks, and the results achieved. Self-efficacy in the context of online education refers to a student's belief in his or her capacity to complete specified learning activities through the use of a learning management system (LMS). A student's attitude toward a learning management system (LMS) is influenced by his or her confidence in his or her ability to use it effectively.

2.2.7. Accessibility

Some universities in rich nations were early adopters of e-learning, particularly with delivery, because it allowed them to attract students who would not otherwise attend higher education and generate revenue for the university. E-learning platforms attract and keep students from a wide range of backgrounds, geographies, experiences, and motivations.

2.2.8. Personal/Individual Factors

Personal qualities and perspectives are examples of individual factors. Adoption of e-learning has been observed to vary by demographic factors like age, gender, major, and years of experience. It has been found that individuals' levels of computer playfulness, computer anxiety, and computer self-efficacy all play a role in how well they adapt to e-learning environments. Research shows that different people respond to e-learning in different ways. Potential adopter traits, such as risk aversion, gender, potential adopter usage style, personal conviction, motivation, experience, self-efficacy, and academic discipline and age, were identified by Grunwald (2002) in a review of the literature on factors that affect the adoption of instructional technology. Personality and/or demographic characteristics (such as features or states of persons, gender, and age) might affect how people view the utility and simplicity of a product. The study found that on an individual level, faculty members' openness to adopting new technologies depends critically on their level of familiarity with and comfort with online content design and development. Acceptance or rejection of e-learning systems by instructors is strongly influenced by both personal opinions and institutional norms. Many professors feel uneasy about their students taking classes online. In particular, they worry that virtual conversations will eventually supplant actual ones. Another worry is that online education will not be an extra option for teachers and pupils but rather a required one. The success of an e-learning program might be hampered by its instructors' and students' mutually mistaken assumptions and interpretations of the technology.

2.2.9. Technical Factors

One of the most influential elements in whether or not educators embrace technological tools for instruction is the accessibility of technical help. This is especially true in the early phases of adopting new technologies. Adoption of e-learning and e-teaching development and delivery is viewed as highly dependent on technical support (Moule *et al.*, 2011). According to Venkatesh (1999), users use anchors like favorable environment and external control to shape their perceptions of how easy it is to use IT. Perceived simplicity is substantially influenced by the presence of external control and by support as a facilitating condition. Those e-learning programs that failed to meet their objectives often lacked the technical guidance and support that helped their peers succeed. Those without enough technological support will be unable to make use of e-learning platforms (Moule *et al.*, 2011). Users' attitudes on the utility and simplicity of use of an e-learning system are influenced by the quality of the technical support provided to them. Technical assistance has been shown to significantly affect the efficiency and usability of an e-learning system (Abbad *et al.*, 2009; Tsuma, 2021).

2.2.10. Flexibility

Students have more control over their learning experience and outcomes when they utilize e-learning. This conclusion was reached after analyzing data from Tsuma (2021), which included enrollment in seventeen open online courses by 841,677 students. The results showed that students used e-learning platforms for many different purposes. Some were students who just wanted to learn, some were students who were teachers looking for resources to use in their classrooms, while others were teachers who were teachers.

2.2.11. Environmental Factors

The industry's size and structure, the number of rivals, the overall economy, and government regulations are all factors that make up the environmental context (Tornatzky & Fleischer, 1990). Other universities, non-governmental organizations (NGOs), governments, and local/national/international ministries all form part of a university's external environment. These groups play a role in shaping how the institution operates. In this way, e-learning uptake is not unique. Educational partners (Islam, 2013) is only one example of a source that highlights environmental concerns related to e-learning adoption.

2.2.12. Technology Factors

These considerations originate from the TAM (Technology Adoption Model). Perceived Usefulness (PU) and Perceived Ease of Use (PEOU) are two key concepts in the TAM, both of which are depicted in the picture (Fig. **1**). Perceived utility, perceived ease of use, and ICT infrastructure are all examples of technological considerations. People's propensity to utilize computers is strongly influenced by their opinion of their usefulness. Perceived ease of use, like attitude and usefulness, has a substantial direct effect on behavioral intention. User adoption of e-learning is greatly influenced by the strength and dependability of the underlying information technology infrastructure. Having more information at one's disposal may increase one's level of skill. According to Lombardi (2007), users' unwillingness to accept and use existing tactics and procedures to acquire the information prevents them from acquiring the capacity to do so. According to Davis (1989), the perceived utility of a method or approach is the degree to which an individual believes that using it will improve his or her performance on the job or in the fulfillment of normal responsibilities. According to his explanation, this viewpoint stems from the assumption that the new skills will improve efficiency. New, innovative technology that is both user-friendly and liberating is more likely to be adopted if its perceived usefulness is high (Pikkarainen *et al.*, 2004). Therefore, it follows that positive attitudes and proven willingness to use e-learning systems will increase in proportion to the perceived utility of such systems. The perceived utility of an e-learning system is positively correlated with the intent to embrace it, according to research (Al-Fraihat *et al.*, 2020). Access to modern information and communication technologies may speed up the spread of online evaluations. However, the absence of information and communication technology (ICT) infrastructures like networks, hardware, software, and power supply is the primary obstacle to the widespread implementation of online assessment around the globe (Bariu, 2020; Masue, 2020).

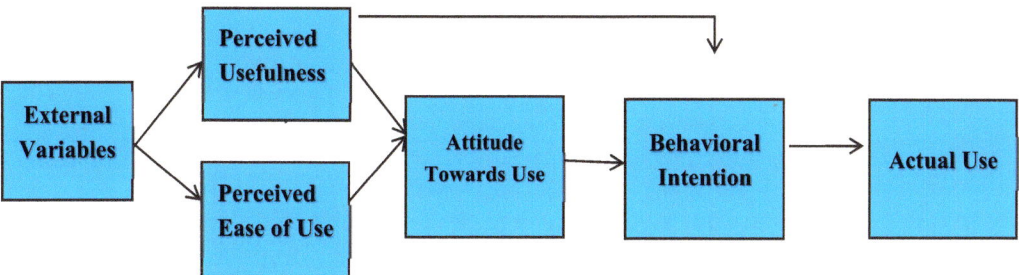

Fig. (1). Technology acceptance model (TAM).
Source: Davis (1989)

An individual's perception of a system's ease of use is the degree to which they believe using that system will be simple and uncomplicated, according to Davis (1989). Therefore, more individuals will adopt and use an app if they believe it to be user-friendly. Perceived Ease of Use, as defined by Zhu, Linb, and Hsu (2012) and elaborated upon by Mohammadi (2015), indicates the extent to which a person believes that employing a given piece of technology would be simple and uncomplicated. Both the system's design and regular use can contribute to the development of users' Information Literacy skills. New technologies are more likely to be adopted and used by the general public if they are intuitive and simple to implement. That is, users are more likely to accept an e-learning system if they believe it is simple to use, and this impression of simplicity might affect how valuable an e-learning system is seen by the user (Mohammadi, 2015). Intention to use (Tarhini *et al.*, 2017) and perceived usefulness (Salloum *et al.*, 2019) are directly influenced by perceived ease of use.

The term "infrastructure" is commonly used to refer to the lowest level of an architectural description or diagram, which includes the physical components of a network as well as the software and procedures used in communications. The importance of networks and connectivity to the growth of functional infrastructure is widely accepted. Nanayakkara (2007) notes that a lack of reliable information and communication networks can negatively affect the distribution of online content to students who are studying from a distance. Tshiningayamwe (2020) found that most institutions had at least the basic information and communication technology (ICT) infrastructure necessary to facilitate distance education. However, more hardware and specialized software are required to construct online courses, such as extra servers and a course administration system. Internet connectivity for students typically involves shared network resources and modems or connections through an ISP. Achieving a high level of dependability from these facilities requires careful management and upkeep. Both the teacher and the student may be reluctant to adopt this technology if the underlying infrastructure is unreliable, underperforming, or untimely supported. Tucker and Gentry (2009) found the same thing, stating that having a solid infrastructure in place is crucial to the successful deployment of e-learning programs and courses.

2.2.13. Smart-Device Use

There has been a small but noticeable uptick in the use of smart gadgets in the workplace, and most companies now permit their use. Smart devices are being used increasingly in numerous fields, including transportation, hospitality, healthcare, and education. All of these industries are making extensive use of these tools in their operations. Using a smart gadget can boost productivity, guaranteeing a return on investment for any business that invests in them. In the manufacturing sector, where it is necessary to manage resources and undertake real-time monitoring of different product stages, IoT devices can be used. Daily routines can also be automated with the help of IoT devices. The gadgets can be used to diagnose technical issues in the system and fix them.

3. DISCUSSION

This chapter looked into what factors influence the uptake of e-learning by both students and teachers. Individual, institutional, and technological barriers to these groups' e-learning adoption were taken into account. Personal qualities and perspectives are examples of individual factors. The adoption of e-learning has been observed to vary by demographic factors like age, gender, major, and years of experience. Individual perceptions of computer playfulness, computer fear, and computer self-efficacy have been identified as factors in e-learning system acceptability (Nanayakkara, 2007). The adoption of e-learning is strongly influenced by institutional context. Users' impressions of the system's utility might be affected by management-supported elements like subjective norms and images. It has been discovered that social influence has a large effect on system usage when usage is mandated but decreases with experience (Nanayakkara & Whiddelt, 2005). Successful adoption of e-learning requires leadership from the top levels of an institution. Adopting e-learning successfully also depends on the school's and institution's overall e-learning strategy. Perceived utility, perceived ease of use, and ICT infrastructure are all examples of technological considerations. People's propensity to utilize computers is strongly influenced by their opinion of their usefulness. Like attitude and usefulness, perceived ease of use has a substantial direct effect on behavioral intention (Davis, 1989). User adoption of e-learning is greatly influenced by the strength and dependability of the underlying information technology infrastructure. The present state of e-learning in universities and the results of previous studies on the topic are also described.

4. IMPLICATIONS

For theoretical purposes, TAM-TEO can be used. The adoption of any modern technology can be explained by the TOE-TAM integrated framework, which takes into account technological, organizational, environmental, and personal factors.

In this research, we used the Technology Acceptance Theory (TAM) and the theory of Planned Behavior (TOE) to create a model for the adoption and implementation of online assessment technologies from the perspectives of both individuals and organizations.

In reality, the odds of e-learning spreading in conventional classrooms have increased as technology has progressed. Students might be motivated to participate in online classes if they have access to a platform that is user- and instructor-friendly.

This research aims to uncover the factors that will help academic institutions and creators of online platforms improve student learning and participation. Our research has theoretical implications for the fields of technology acceptance modeling (TAM) and technology, organization, and environment (TEO). Researchers can now use these findings as guides for further improving the TAM and applying it to e-learning adoption studies, which will ultimately strengthen the model's theoretical underpinnings.

An e-learning policy can help ensure that all relevant parties are properly brought into the fold to maximize the effectiveness of the platform. Once again, the policy's framework should account for the varying factors that influence adoption among the various stakeholders. The entire implementation of e-learning will be facilitated by this all-encompassing strategy, so stakeholders will utilize the system for more than just checking grades. E-learning is not only a fad but rather an integral part of today's formal education and business training. The effectiveness and interest of online training programs depend on constant upkeep and evaluation. The perceived usefulness and the intention to utilize an e-learning system are both affected by the system's perceived ease of use. This suggests that students will be motivated to adopt e-learning platforms once they have a firm grasp on the relative ease of using them. In addition, students may have a positive attitude toward the use of an e-learning system if the system's graphic interface is created with user-friendly functions, website navigation, frequently asked questions, and user instructions. Because of this, they will be more or less likely to adopt and benefit from e-learning systems. System quality, service quality, information quality, and perceived utility have all been found to play significant roles in determining whether or not users adopt a given technology. Designers of the e-learning platform should give this consideration if they want to boost user uptake. Additionally, the system interfaces need to be more intuitive and easier for people with even rudimentary IT knowledge to utilize. The adoption rate can be increased by giving both students and teachers the necessary resources and training. The intricacy of e-learning-related concerns, such as enhancing the IT literacy of trainers and designers and developing intricate digital curricula for universities, must also be taken into account. Without cooperation across sectors like academics, instructional designers and learning practitioners, and IT- and platform providers, the lofty objective of realizing the complete implementation of digital curriculum will not become a reality. Trainers and course designers need not only the knowledge and experience to employ technology in the classroom but also the motivation to do so. Their undivided attention, dedication, effort, and expertise are indispensable. For the digital curriculum to be effectively presented and implemented, trainers need access to professional development programs that give them the technical skills and pedagogical expertise they need to do so.

The study also found that how comfortable a student feels with using a computer is a major factor in how they evaluate the benefits and convenience of an e-learning system. One of the most important factors in a student's recognition of the value of e-learning is the student's belief in his or her competence to use or run an e-learning system *via* a computer system. This necessitates that schools provide students with ongoing information and communication technology (ICT) instruction to ensure they graduate with the necessary proficiency. Students' perceptions of e-learning's value and convenience are likely to be enhanced after participating in such training sessions, which can increase their comfort level with using various computer-related apps. In other words, students' perceptions of the value of and comfort with using an e-learning system will be shaped by the level of instruction they receive on computers.

CONCLUSION

The primary purpose of this research is to examine the elements that contribute to the positive reception of e-learning by educators and learners. The benefits of technology can only be realized if people utilize it, according to the results of previous studies in the field of technology adoption study. The dissemination of knowledge, the conduct of research, and the conduct of international communication have all been profoundly affected by technological advancements. Modern technology has made it possible for universities to teach anyone, anywhere in the world, regardless of their location. More and more schools are seeing the benefits of incorporating technology into the classroom. This rapid pace of period integration has provided higher education with a model to explore innovative methods of instruction. This research synthesis looks at the literature on the value of ICT in higher education and how it affects students at different levels of education. Because technology has become a tool that promotes access and use of up-to-date information resources to increase productivity and development, it must be used correctly in today's ever-evolving information environment. The TAM model is used in this article to explain why and how educational institutions should adopt new technologies.

RECOMMENDATIONS

The vice chancellor, pro vice chancellors, principals, deans, and directors of a university may need to attend a sensitization session to fully grasp the significance of e-learning. The upper echelons of management will be better able to teach their employees, and provide incentives, time off to produce e-learning modules, help desk support, and ICT support as a result. Therefore, upper management must allot more funds to support the system's use, hire more people to staff the help desk and hire system administrators and instructional designers to train professors to create and distribute online content. Faculty adoption of the system can be facilitated by offering incentives. This encompasses both monetary compensation and public acknowledgment for creating and educating with online information. Because of this, e-learning will have greater backing from upper management and be more widely used. All university professors should be required to participate in a program to improve their computer skills and learn how to use a learning management system (LMS). This will increase comfort with and enjoyment of using computers, as well as decrease stress over using them. Usability will also be improved. All of this will ultimately result in more people using e-learning. Access to the internet for fast and stable connections, a more user-friendly learning management system, and a separate, replicated server are all essential components of a successful e-learning infrastructure. To increase accessibility and decrease maintenance, the ICT division should put more money into high-speed internet. The e-learning platform should be hosted on a separate, dedicated server, which should be replicated by the IT department in case of data loss. The alternative would be to investigate other low-cost solutions, such as cloud hosting.

REFERENCES

Al-Ghurbani, A. M., Jazima, F., Abdulrab, M., Al-Mamaryc, H. Y. S., Khan, I. (2022). The Impact of Internal Factors on the Use of Technology in Higher Education in Saudi Arabia during the COVID-19 Pandemic *Human Systems Management* IOS Press.

Abbad, M.M., Morris, D., De Nahlik, C. (2009). Looking under the bonnet: Factors affecting student adoption of e-learning systems in Jordan. *Int. Rev. Res. Open Distance Learn.*, *10*(2), 1-16.

[http://dx.doi.org/10.19173/irrodl.v10i2.596]

Al-Fraihat, D., Joy, M., Masa'deh, R., Sinclair, J. (2020). Evaluating E-learning systems success: An empirical study. *Comput. Human Behav., 102*, 67-86.
[http://dx.doi.org/10.1016/j.chb.2019.08.004]

Aparicio, M., Bacao, F., Oliveira, T. (2016). An e-learning theoretical framework. *J. Educ. Technol. Syst., 19*(1), 292-307.

Al-Rahmi, W.M., Alias, N., Othman, M.S., Alzahrani, A.I., Alfarraj, O., Saged, A.A., Abdul Rahman, N.S. (2018). Use of e-learning by university students in Malaysian higher educational institutions: A case in Universiti Teknologi Malaysia. *IEEE Access, 6*, 14268-14276.
[http://dx.doi.org/10.1109/ACCESS.2018.2802325]

Bandura, A. (1977). Self-efficacy: Toward a unifying theory of behavioral change. *Psychol. Rev., 84*(2), 191-215.
[http://dx.doi.org/10.1037/0033-295X.84.2.191] [PMID: 847061]

Bariu, T.N. (2020). Status of ICT Infrastructure Used in Teaching and Learning in Secondary Schools in Meru County, Kenya. *European Journal of Interactive Multimedia and Education, 1*(1), e02002.
[http://dx.doi.org/10.30935/ejimed/8283]

Davis, F.D. (1986). A technology acceptance model for empirically testing new end-user information systems: Theory and results. *Thesis: Doctoral dissertation, Sloan School of Management, Massachusetts Institute of Technology.*

Davis, F.D. (1989). Perceived usefulness, perceived ease of use, and user acceptance of information technology. *Manage. Inf. Syst. Q., 13*(3), 319-340.
[http://dx.doi.org/10.2307/249008]

Davis, F.D., Bagozzi, R.P., Warshaw, P.R. (1989). User acceptance of computer technology: a comparison of two theoretical models. *Manage. Sci., 35*(8), 982-1003.
[http://dx.doi.org/10.1287/mnsc.35.8.982]

Fishbein, M., Ajzen, I. (1975). *Belief, attitude, intention and behavior: An introduction to theory and research..* Reading, MA: Addison-Wesley.

Grunwald, H. (2002). *Factors Affecting Faculty Adoption and Sustained Use of Instructional Technology in Traditional Classrooms. Comprehensive Qualifying Exam..* Center for the Study of Higher and Postsecondary Education, University of Michigan.

Islam, A.K.M.N. (2013). Investigating e-learning system usage outcomes in the university context. *Comput. Educ., 69*, 387-399.
[http://dx.doi.org/10.1016/j.compedu.2013.07.037]

Kjellsdotter, A. (2020). What matter(s)? A didactical analysis of primary school teachers' ICT integration. *J. Curric. Stud., 52*(6), 823-839.
[http://dx.doi.org/10.1080/00220272.2020.1759144]

Lombardi, M.M. (2007). Authentic Learning for the 21st Century: An Overview. Educare Learning Initiative. Available from: https://net.educause.edu/ir/library/pdf/ELI3009.pdf

Mubarak Al-Awidi, H., M Aldhafeeri, F. (2017). Teachers' Readiness to Implement Digital Curriculum in Kuwaiti Schools. *J. Inf. Technol. Educ., 16*, 105-126.
[http://dx.doi.org/10.28945/3685]

Mohamad Hsbollah, H., Kamil, (2009). E-learning adoption: the role of relative advantages, trialability and academic specialisation. *Campus-Wide Inf. Syst., 26*(1), 54-70.
[http://dx.doi.org/10.1108/10650740910921564]

Masue, O.S. (2020). Applicability of E-learning in Higher Learning Institutions in Tanzania Willy A. *Innocent Mbeya University of Science and Technology, Tanzania, 16*(2), 242-249. Available from: https://eric.ed.gov/?id=EJ1268804

Mohammadi, H. (2015). Investigating users' perspectives on e-learning: An integration of TAM and IS success model. *Comput. Human Behav., 45*, 359-374.
[http://dx.doi.org/10.1016/j.chb.2014.07.044]

Moule, P., Ward, R., Lockyer, L. (2011). Issues with e-learning in nursing and health education in the UK: are new technologies being embraced in the teaching and learning environments? *J. Res. Nurs., 16*(1), 77-90.
[http://dx.doi.org/10.1177/1744987110370940]

Memon, A.B., Meyer, K. (2017). Why we need dedicated web-based collaboration platforms for inter-organizational connectivity? A research synthesis. *International Journal of Information Technology and Computer Science, 9*(11), 1-11.
[http://dx.doi.org/10.5815/ijitcs.2017.11.01]

Martins, J., Branco, F., Gonçalves, R., Au-Yong-Oliveira, M., Oliveira, T., Naranjo-Zolotov, M., Cruz-Jesus, F. (2019). Assessing the success behind the use of education management information systems in higher education. *Telemat. Inform., 38*, 182-193.
[http://dx.doi.org/10.1016/j.tele.2018.10.001]

Nanayakkara, C. (2007). A Model of User Acceptance of Learning Management Systems. *Int. J. Learn., 12*(12), 223-232.
[http://dx.doi.org/10.18848/1447-9494/CGP/v13i12/45146]

Nanayakkara, C., Whiddelt, R.J. (2005). A Model of User Acceptance of Learning Management Systems: a Case Study of a Polytechnic in New Zealand. *Information Systems Technology and its Applications* (pp. 180-190). Palmerston North.

Namisiko, P., Munialo, C., Nyongesa, S. (2014). Towards an Optimization Framework for E-learning in Developing Countries: A Case of Private Universities in Kenya. *Journal of Computer Science and Information Technology, 2*(2), 131-148.

Nkhoma, M.Z., Dang, D.P.T. (2013). Contributing Factors of Cloud Computing Adoption: a Technology-Organisation-Environment Framework Approach. *International Journal of Information Systems and Engineering, 1*(1), 30-41.
[http://dx.doi.org/10.24924/ijise/2013.04/v1.iss1/30.41]

OECD. (2005). E-learning in Tertiary Education. Policy Brief. Available from: http://www.oecd.org/internet/35961132.pdf

Pikkarainen, T., Pikkarainen, K., Karjaluoto, H., Pahnila, S. (2004). Consumer acceptance of online banking: an extension of the technology acceptance model. *Internet Res., 14*(3), 224-235.
[http://dx.doi.org/10.1108/10662240410542652]

Salloum, S.A., Al-Emran, M., Habes, M., Alghizzawi, M., Ghani, M.A., Shaalan, K. (2019). Understanding the impact of social media practices on e-learning systems acceptance [Paper presentation]. *International Conference on Advanced Intelligent Systems and Informatics.* October 19–21 Cairo, Egypt

Salloum, S.A., Qasim Mohammad Alhamad, A., Al-Emran, M., Abdel Monem, A., Shaalan, K. (2019). Exploring students' acceptance of e-learning through the development of a comprehensive technology acceptance model. *IEEE Access, 7*, 128445-128462.
[http://dx.doi.org/10.1109/ACCESS.2019.2939467]

Singh, V., Thurman, A. (2019). How many ways can we define online learning? A systematic literature review of definitions of online learning (1988-2018). *Am. J. Distance Educ., 33*(4), 289-306.
[http://dx.doi.org/10.1080/08923647.2019.1663082]

Tshiningayamwe, S. (2020). The Shifts to Online Learning: Assumptions, Implications and Possibilities for Quality Education in Teacher Education. *Southern African Journal of Environmental Education., 36*(March), 16-33.
[http://dx.doi.org/10.4314/sajee.v36i3.16]

Tarman, B. (2017). Editorial: The Future of Social Sciences. *Research in Social Sciences and Technology, 2*(2), I-VI. Available from: http://ressat.org/index.php/ressat/article/view/329

Tarman, B. (2016). Innovation and Education. *Research in Social Sciences and Technology, 1*(1), 77-97. [http://dx.doi.org/10.46303/ressat.01.01.4]

Tarman, B., Chigisheva, O. (2017). Transformation of educational policy, theory and practice in post-soviet social studies education. *Journal of Social Studies Education Research, 8*(2), I-IV. [Editorial].

Tarhini, A., Hone, K., Liu, X., Tarhini, T. (2017). Examining the moderating effect of individual-level cultural values on users' acceptance of E-learning in developing countries: a structural equation modeling of an extended technology acceptance model. *Interact. Learn. Environ., 25*(3), 306-328. [http://dx.doi.org/10.1080/10494820.2015.1122635]

Tsuma, K. (2021). Students' Use of e-Learning Platforms. *Social Science Journal for Advanced Research, 1*(3), 15-25. [http://dx.doi.org/10.54741/ssjar.1.3.3]

Wood, R., Bandura, A. (1989). Social cognitive theory of organizational management. *Acad. Manage. Rev., 14*(3), 361-384. [http://dx.doi.org/10.2307/258173]

Zhang, Z., Cao, T., Shu, J., Liu, H. (2020). Identifying key factors affecting college students' adoption of the e-learning system in mandatory blended learning environments. *Interact. Learn. Environ., 30*(8), 1-14.

CHAPTER 5

The Adoption of Artificial Intelligence in the Education Sector

Abstract: The objective of this chapter is to elucidate the integration of artificial intelligence (AI) within the education sector while also examining the advantages of AI in education based on existing scholarly literature. Artificial intelligence (AI) addresses various contemporary difficulties in the field of education, including bridging the technological divide between learners and educators, ensuring trustworthy and ethical learning systems, facilitating distance learning, and advancing the development of high-quality data as well as solutions for the current educational process. The potential implications of artificial intelligence (AI) in the field of education are vast, as this technology has the capability to effectively address various challenges within the online education system.

Keywords: Adoption, Artificial intelligence, Education, Students, Sector technology.

1. INTRODUCTION

While Artificial Intelligence (AI) has emerged as a game-changing technology, its potential applications in the classroom have been largely ignored. This is not surprising given that education is predicated on interpersonal skill sets (knowledge exchange and communication) that do not necessitate the use of artificial intelligence.

There has been a recent spate of papers discussing the benefits of artificial intelligence in the classroom, but most of them center on the students rather than the teachers. No industry is immune to the transformative power of artificially intelligent technology (AI), and education is no exception.

In the next three years, up to 47% of learning management products will have artificial intelligence features, according to the education industry. Although AI-driven solutions have been available in EdTech for some years, widespread adoption has been gradual (Karandish, 2021). But the pandemic changed everything, and teachers had to rely on online education.

Abdul-Mumin Khalid & Obeng Owusu-Boateng
All rights reserved-© 2024 Bentham Science Publishers

Eighty-six percent of teachers now believe that technological advancements should be incorporated into every aspect of classroom instruction. Artificial intelligence has the potential to enhance the educational experience for students and faculty alike. Importantly, AI offers some novel possibilities for incremental improvements in the classroom. When added up and considered over a longer period, these small improvements can have a major impact on outcomes like student engagement and performance.

AI can also be utilized to aid educators, streamline processes and offer timely insights that will make their jobs easier overall. AI, or artificial intelligence, is the process of programming a computer to mimic human intelligence and behavior. It is a method for programming computers to mimic human thought processes. The purpose of AI is to perform like a human being. Artificial intelligence (AI) has several potential applications in the field of education, among others.

The use of AI to solve problems like language processing, reasoning, planning, and cognitive modeling is increasing the demand for technology in the classroom. As Majeed (2023) points out, AI can help with the synthesis and structuring of knowledge to enable the dissemination of content in a different learning method. There is a wide range of reactions to the prospect of using AI in the classroom, from exhilaration to worry to a slew of unanswered concerns. Some people are hopeful that AI will revolutionize classroom instruction, while others are worried about the dangers it could pose to society. In recent years, the education sector has attracted increased attention from AI developers because of the widespread impact of AI applications in this area. One of the most significant trends in education is the increased use of information and communication technology and its applications (Educause, 2021). Learning and teaching are only two areas where AI is finding more and more uses in the educational sector. Horizon Research predicted a 43% growth in AI applications between 2018 and 2022. The same group's analysis expected an even larger increase in the use of AI technology than had previously been seen (Educause, 2021). The future of AI and its function in education are inextricably connected (Ahmad *et al.*, 2021). Artificial intelligence (AI) is here to stay, and there are already tools available to help teachers use it effectively in the classroom. In this piece, we will look at what AI is, how it can help schools, and what problems it can solve.

2. LITERATURE

2.1. Artificial Intelligence (AI)

AI is a technology that can reason, understand human language, and do tasks such as resolving complicated problems, diagnosing medical conditions, and maintaining vehicle functionality. It can acquire unfamiliar languages, execute chess, and paint impressionist-style imitations. An AI system, or a computerized intelligence system, is a sort of computer software that can perform tasks often performed by intelligent humans (Majeed, 2023). It is important to stop thinking about AI as a singular technique and instead view it as an umbrella word that encompasses several different technologies and techniques, such as NLP, NN, DM, ML, and algorithms (Baker & Smith, 2019). Artificial intelligence is the capability of machines to do tasks normally associated with human or animal intelligence. It is the practice of teaching computers to solve issues and make judgments autonomously using only the massive amounts of unstructured data already available, such as text and images. There is no denying the impact of fields like philosophy, economics, neurology, and cognitive science on the field of artificial intelligence (Zawacki-Richter *et al.*, 2019), even though its origins can be traced back to computer science and engineering. Systems with AI capabilities may recognize patterns in data, learn from new data, and correct mistakes, allowing them to perform jobs that previously required human intellect. Because this definition of intelligence is both very broad and awkwardly tautological, artificial intelligence is typically described as the practice of making machines that can accurately respond to and anticipate changes in their immediate surroundings (Tuomi, 2018). The application of AI to the subject of education has been revolutionary because of the emphasis it places on achieving concrete outcomes.

2.2. Adoption of AI in the Education Sector

According to a study by Hamdan (2017), the use of AI in the classroom can help teachers save time and money by allowing them to better utilize digital resources and cutting-edge online platforms. Recent research has produced an Artificial Intelligence Teaching System (AITS) that electronically assesses student achievement (Majeed, 2023). The system's ability to instruct and absorb knowledge of search strategies is useful for both students and instructors. The results of the algorithm were found to be highly comparable to those of human tutors, according to an analysis of 400 evaluations. Since AI-assisted evaluation allows students to better comprehend their learning and do it in a timely and correct manner, it may lead to a fresh crop of more inspired learners (Luckin, 2017). The possibility that computers might one day replace humans as educators is a major concern in the field of artificial intelligence research (Humble & Mozelius, 2019). To prepare for the future, governments and countries must develop a profile of the ideal educator who can integrate with these systems of support (Wogu, Misra, Olu-Owolabi, Assibong, & Udoh, 2018). Professors can transcribe their lectures with the help of a voice-to-text tool. Students are expected to do some pre-lecture reading and to have questions ready; alternatively, they can follow along and take notes during the lecture without trying to record every word. The impact of technology on the classroom cannot be overstated. Using natural language processing (NLP), artificial intelligence (AI) can facilitate testing in a manner analogous to plagiarism detection. If you want to save even more time, you can just stick the scanner right into the scanner machine. Teachers are optimistic that AI can streamline their daily operations and improve their pupils' access to timely feedback. Grammarly, Wordsense, and Turnitin are just some of the anti-plagiarism tools that have been used by teachers for years. Teachers discourage plagiarism because it reflects poorly on their pupils (Gupta, 2023) and themselves. Some innovative preemptive educational systems are being developed to combat plagiarism.

2.3. Benefits of AI Adoption in the Education Sector

Students who need additional assistance beyond school hours are quite rare, but many educators simply do not have the time to provide it. Chatbots and online tutors driven by artificial intelligence appear to be the way to go in these situations. AI programs can help students practice skills and improve weaker areas even when they are not in class (Karandish, 2021). However, no chatbot has yet shown the potential to replace a teacher. They provide pupils more freedom to learn at their own pace, but the teacher is not always there to help. A chatbot driven by AI can respond to student inquiries in 2.7 seconds or less (Karandish, 2021).

- **Identifying Risk Factors**

Keeping a light footprint through distance learning is one of the major advantages of AI technology in the classroom. Many specialists, nevertheless, anticipate that AI will shortly supplant human teachers. Together, AI and education can supplement traditional and online modes of instruction. By automating several activities and enhancing the process of instruction and learning for individuals, AI can assist specialists (Gupta, 2023) in their endeavors.

- **Tutoring**

Personal study plans are constantly updated to account for students' areas of weakness that can be addressed through individualized instruction. Students who have access to private tutors and extra support outside of class are more likely to succeed and avoid frustrating their parents with mathematics questions. Teachers can save a lot of time with the help of AI tutors because they do not have to spend as much time on individual students. Students no longer have to feel awkward about needing extra assistance in class thanks to chatbots and other AI-powered virtual personal assistants.

- **Learning Excellence**

AI can monitor and assess how different students learn and retain information. AI puts students' knowledge to use, evaluates their aptitude for learning, and continues teaching them in real time. It allows teachers to adapt their approaches to a wide range of students while still using the same materials and techniques. According to a large body of evidence, kids who receive their education in this format show considerable improvement in their academic performance compared to those who receive it in the more conventional classroom setting. Education based on artificial intelligence also makes it possible to provide a high-quality education to everyone. It does more than just boost the effectiveness of test-focused education; it also incorporates features like critical thinking instruction and innovation skill development to fully grow students' potential.

- **Encourage Discussion and Interaction between Instructors and Students**

Building rapport with students and expressing oneself are crucial components of teaching. The result is a classroom where students are comfortable speaking up, asking questions, sharing ideas, and voicing concerns—an environment where they may develop their soft skills alongside their mastery of the course material. Relationship building between instructors and students can be aided by the use of AI in the classroom. For instance, if the classroom is set up properly, interruptions in conversation and a failure to retain information are less likely to occur. The same holds for classroom instructors; if students express confusion, the teacher will know to either clarify the material or provide opportunities for them to put it into practice (Plitnichenko, 2020). Artificial intelligence in the classroom can learn to recognize patterns of student confusion over time, allowing educators to better adapt their methods.

- **Reduced Stress**

Students can avoid comparing themselves to one another when they get instruction that is adapted to their own learning needs. Earlier, a pupil would be required to raise his hand in front of the whole class and request assistance (Plitnichenko, 2020). It is now sufficient to type a question into a virtual assistant and receive an immediate response (Plitnichenko, 2020). There is less stress in the classroom because of the chances presented by AI tools that highlight individual growth. With less stress and more motivation to learn, students can focus better.

- **Collaborative Education**

One of the many educational opportunities and benefits offered by artificial intelligence is immersive learning. Therefore, students are given more control over their learning and are exposed to real-world experiences they may apply outside of the classroom. Education will be affected by the exponential development of AI in our society, especially when you consider how unadaptable humans are about AI's capacity to absorb information at lightning speed while doing precise computations without committing errors or tiring out.

• Informational Structuring

In addition to the potential of AI-based educational systems, there are many ways in which students can benefit from artificial intelligence. Teachers and educators all around the world have made use of smart gadgets' excellent capabilities, such as their ability to continuously feed knowledge from a range of sources to improve their students' academic outcomes. As a result of their superior comprehension and speed of application, AI technologies are also finding widespread use in classrooms around the world.

• Construct More Eeffective Lessons in Less Time

Lesson preparation can be a tedious procedure, especially if it must be done outside of working hours. It is expected that teachers will require time to carefully organize lessons to ensure they are comprehensive, age-appropriate, and consistent with the overall curriculum (Majeed, 2023). Artificial intelligence is also beginning to show promise in this crucial area. The process of lesson planning can be made easier and more effective by automating some of the more repetitive or predictable procedures involved. In addition, AI can help improve the quality of lessons itself.

• Intelligent Content Generation

Gupta (2023) argues that AI and ML can assist educators and researchers in developing cutting-edge materials for more accessible teaching and study. AI smart content production enhances the real-world experience of visible web-based study environments, which traditional teaching approaches cannot deliver outside of lab experiments. The technology facilitates 2D-3D visualization, allowing for many modes of information perception in the classroom. AI in the classroom can facilitate bite-size learning *via* low-storage digital course materials and other instructional resources. In this approach, everyone from freshmen to seasoned researchers can benefit from the full breadth of available resources. Furthermore, these resources will be available across multiple platforms, making distance education a non-issue. Artificial intelligence also makes it easier for people to develop and update content often, which helps maintain training materials. Users are also alerted if any new data is added, allowing them to better prepare for prospective endeavors.

• **Learning Opportunities**

Online AI tutors ensure students never miss a class. They can arrange their day as they like without being constrained by location. They are free to study whenever and wherever they like. Based on this information, they can arrange their timetable accordingly.

• **Personalization**

Educators and students alike gain from this. Personalizing lessons for each learner is a major debate in the field of education today. With the help of AI, today's students can engage in individualized learning that takes into account their prior knowledge and personal interests. Learning gaps can be identified and filled with the use of artificial intelligence, which also creates a custom study plan for each student. Artificial intelligence makes learning more efficient by adapting to each individual's demands. AI has the potential to personalize the learning experience for each student by taking into account their prior knowledge, learning speed, and intended learning results. Solutions powered by AI can also examine a student's learning history to spot trouble spots and advise on which classes would be the most beneficial for them to progress in. To the same extent that AI can tailor students' distance-learning experiences, it can also do so for educators. With the use of AI, courseware may be tailored to each student's unique needs (Gupta, 2023) and learning style. In addition, the system reinforces the student's understanding of the material and adjusts to their learning style to lessen the load. This integration of AI and education caters to the needs of each learner by providing tools such as AI-enhanced games, individualized curriculums, and more. AI can assist educators in determining which concepts and lessons should be reviewed. This data can help educators tailor their lessons to the needs of individual students. To prevent pupils from falling behind, educators must assess their students' learning gaps and adapt their curricula accordingly (Gupta, 2023). Algorithms that use artificial intelligence to make subject recommendations can look at students' historical data to determine, for example, which subjects each student excels in and which ones they struggle with.

• **Using Robots**

Using the computational power of AI, routine operations like grading papers and testing learning patterns can be automated. Time-consuming operations like grading, assessing, and responding to students might be streamlined with the help of AI to save teachers time. Manual tasks can be automated with the use of support automation systems, freeing up valuable classroom time (Haroon, 2023) for the instruction of fundamental skills. An AI-driven solution may scan student test papers using natural language processing algorithms, identify and analyze proper responses to questions, and assign grades to students accordingly. Any educational institution can take advantage of AI technology to automate the aforementioned processes. These AI solutions examine student performance data to determine where pupils are struggling and offer advice on how to help them succeed. AI can help teachers create engaging lessons by enhancing their use of visuals and motion. To provide the greatest possible education for children, schools of all sizes must adopt AI solutions.

- **Stronger Participation**

Each student has a unique learning experience thanks to AI that tailors their schedule, assignments, interactions with digital tools, and suggestions to their specific needs. In addition, making pupils feel like individuals has been shown to increase their involvement and enthusiasm in school (Plitnichenko, 2020).

- **Made-to-Order Digital Textbooks**

AI algorithms are the best-fit solution to this particular snag because they can create softcopy by extracting data from scanned hardcopy, the internet, and recent research published for a specific subject or topic (Gupta, 2023) without the need for extensive manual labor or research.

- **AI-Based Testing**

Artificial intelligence software systems can be actively employed in interviews and tests to help spot suspect behavior and notify the supervisor. Through the use of keystroke analysis and monitoring *via* web cameras, microphones, and browsers, the AI systems can maintain tabs on every person. As one of the most reliable options for online testing, this AI technology benefits education and has been widely adopted (Gupta, 2023) in higher education. There are countless uses for software and apps powered by artificial intelligence.

- **Reactions to Queries**

Chatbots powered by AI that have access to a school's entire knowledge base can answer students' most frequently asked questions without involving a human instructor. AI eliminates the need for teachers to perform routine tasks, so they have more time to focus on things like lesson planning, curriculum research, and increasing student engagement (Karandish, 2021).

- **Coaching**

Many educators do not have time to meet the needs of their pupils who require supplemental instruction on weekends or after school when they are homeschooled. Artificially intelligent teachers and chatbots are the best answers here (Majeed, 2023) for a variety of reasons. Chatbots cannot take the role of human educators, but there are AI resources that can help students work on their weak spots outside of the classroom. With the support of AI, students and tutors can work together independently at any time of day or night (Haroon, 2023) for a truly personalized education. In as little as 5 seconds, a chatbot powered by AI can provide a solution to a student's query.

• **Quick to Respond**

Frustration sets in when a question is asked and answered three days later (Haroon, 2023) than expected. The academics and staff are often asked the same things. Using AI's conversational intelligence and support automation, instructors may respond to student inquiries in a couple of seconds. This helps both students and teachers by reducing the amount of time spent searching for information.

• **Persistent Backing**

Thanks to AI-driven resources, education is accessible to students everywhere, at any time. Students can experiment with different approaches whenever they like without waiting for clearance from their teachers. As a result, students from all around the world can obtain access to high-quality education without paying travel or living fees (Haroon, 2023).

• **Personalized Analysis Based on Your Data**

Whether in the classroom or on the job, feedback is an essential component of effective learning design. Effective teaching differs significantly from merely disseminating information in that it involves regular feedback to students. Artificial intelligence (AI) in the classroom uses ordinary data to assess and determine work reports, ensuring that only reliable sources are used. A data-driven feedback system improves student engagement, eliminates prejudice in the classroom, and reveals skill gaps. Each employee and student's feedback is customized based on their performance data.

2.4. Future of Artificial Intelligence in the Educational Sector

Teachers will always be indispensable, but the demands placed on them in the modern educational system may be different. We have previously established that AI has the potential to automate a variety of functions, including grading, reports, assisting students while studying, and even serving as a viable alternative to a human tutor in some circumstances. The use of artificial intelligence in education can take several forms. In the future, AI systems may replace teachers in the classroom by answering students' questions and clearing up their misconceptions about fundamental concepts. In these situations, AI has the potential to transform the educator into a facilitator. Voice-to-text functionality is now standard on most smartphones and several home gadgets. But what if we do not stop at scheduling tasks and placing food orders? The use of speech-to-text (STT) technologies is made possible by machine learning. How students learn and do research may be profoundly affected by innovations such as natural language processing (NLP) and automatic voice recognition (ASR). With the help of automated speech recognition (ASR) technology, transcripts of any audio or video can be generated mechanically. Possible applications of natural language processing in the classroom include summarization, theme extraction, and monitoring student engagement. The use of technology in the classroom opens up a world of knowledge to students. College prep courses instill in pupils the value of narrowing their focus. When machine learning is utilized to supplement classroom instruction, AI has access to a broader pool of data from which to learn. Integrating improvements to learning is possible. Accuracy is essential even when using AI for education. Teachers are always pushing themselves, even with the aid of AI, to come up with fresh and engaging content.

3. IMPLICATIONS

Students who receive additional training can help firms close the technology divide. Opportunities for students to acquire new skills are readily available and inexpensive thanks to AI and ML-powered software and application development solutions. Training and education programs for employees already working in a company can have the same effect as those for students, boosting morale and igniting a company-wide dedication to improvement and innovation. In addition, Deep Learning and Machine Learning for Education affect the L&D (Learning and Development) field through research on the processes through which individuals gain knowledge. Once the technology learns how humans learn best, it will automate the learning process to match those preferences. Students can learn the basics using these AI tools, but they are not designed to teach complex ideas. Students still need a lecturer to help them understand these kinds of intricate ideas. Complex problems that call for analytical thinking and reasoning are currently beyond the capabilities of AI, but this may change in the future.

CONCLUSION

There has been some pushback to integrating AI into classrooms, and the topic of how AI can be used by students continues to dominate conversations. However, AI has the potential to help educators in significant ways as well. For educators, this means a better ability to respond at the moment to students' learning requirements, more effective communication, and more efficient lesson preparation. After all, AI already drives many of the market's most popular software products, and it can be found in other examples of technology we use every day. Machine learning is used to speed up tasks, increase precision, derive insights from data, and personalize the user experience. Producing intelligent content (e.g., question papers, learning material) is one of the most significant uses of AI in education, with the potential to revolutionize the sector as a whole. AI has the potential to generate question papers quickly and accurately, freeing up valuable time for educators. Digital textbooks and study aids can be created by AI algorithms as well. As a result of the benefits they offer in terms of ease of understanding and idea visualization, simulation and visualization-based learning have recently gained in popularity. The prevalence and use of AI continue to expand across numerous industries. Artificial intelligence (AI) has begun to exhibit its effects in the sector of education, where it is functioning as a helpful tool for both students and teachers and assisting the learning process. However, not all universities have fully used AI in the classroom yet, and doing so will be a lengthy process. However, research indicates that AI will soon have a positive effect on the academic world. It is already revolutionizing the sector but has not yet lived up to its promise in classrooms. Computer-based learning has many advantages, but it will probably never completely replace human instructors in educational institutions.

REFERENCES

Ahmad, S.F., Rahmat, M.K., Mubarik, M.S., Alam, M.M., Hyder, S.I. (2021). Artificial Intelligence and Its Role in Education. *Sustainability (Basel), 13*(22), 12902.
[http://dx.doi.org/10.3390/su132212902]

Baker, R.S. (2016). Stupid tutoring systems, intelligent humans. *Int. J. Artif. Intell. Educ., 26*(2), 600-614.
[http://dx.doi.org/10.1007/s40593-016-0105-0]

EDUCAUSE. (2019). Higher Education Edition. Retrieved from EDUCAUSE Learning Initiative and The New Media Consortium. Available Online: https://library.educause.edu/-/media/files/library/2019/4/2019horizonreport.pdf (Accessed on: 19 April 2021).

Gupta, D. (2023). Top 10 Ways AI in Education is Transforming the Industry. Available from: https://appinventiv.com/blog/10-ways-artificial-intelligence-transforming-the-education-industry/

Haroon, H. (2023). Benefits of Artificial Intelligence In Education. Edifying World. Available from: https://www.edifyingworld.com/2022/03/ai-education.html

Karandish, D. (2021). 7 benefits of AI in education. Available from: https://thejournal.com/articles/2021/06/23/7-benefits-of-ai-in-education.aspx

Majeed, M. (2023). Opportunities and Challenges Associated with Online/Blended Teaching-Learning. *Digital Transformation in Education: Emerging Markets and Opportunities, 2023*(1), 98-117.
[http://dx.doi.org/10.2174/9789815124750123010010]

Majeed, M. (2023). Predicting the Future of Education in the Light of Artificial Intelligence. *Digital Transformation in Education: Emerging Markets and Opportunities, 2023*(1), 173-188.
[http://dx.doi.org/10.2174/9789815124750123010014]

Plitnichenko, L. (2020). 5 Main Roles of Artificial Intelligence In Education. Available from: https://elearningindustry.com/5-main-roles-artificial-intelligence-in-education

Wogu, I.A.P., Misra, S., Olu-Owolabi, E.F., Assibong, P.A., Udoh, O.D. (2018). Artificial intelligence, artificial teachers and the fate of learners in the 21st century education sector: Implications for theory and practice. *Int. J. Pure Appl. Math.,* *119*(16), 2245-2259.

Zawacki-Richter, O., Marín, V., Bond, M., Gouverneur, F. (2019). Systematic review of research on artificial intelligence applications in higher education – where are the educators? *Int J Educ Technol High Educ,* *16*(1), 1-27.

CHAPTER 6

The Adoption of Big Data in the Education Sector

Abstract: Big Data enables higher educational institutions the ability to efficiently use information technology resources to enhance the effectiveness of education and performance. This chapter explores the meaning of big data applicable to educational institutions, identifies the factors that affect the adoption of big data approach in higher education institutions, especially for strategic management purposes and aims to examine the challenges of adopting big data in higher education institutions. The literature sources are from journals on scientific studies and articles, and research papers. The benefits of BD in the education sector include academic productivity, teaching efficiency, organization of processes, freedom of tech stack/tech stack independence, reduction in student dropout, managing the business's finances and operations, maintaining open and honest communication, multiplication of data, accelerating the instructional process and personalization. The driving factors are the TEO framework (organizational, technological and environmental), *etc.*

Keywords: Big data, Colleges, Education, Learners, Students, Technology, Teachers, Universities.

1. INTRODUCTION

As new technologies arise, the world quickly adapts to accommodate them. Many people today rely on various pieces of technology (Shorfuzzaman, Hossain, Nazir, Muhammad, & Alamri, 2019).

Every second, these gadgets generate a staggering amount of data (ur Rehman *et al.*, 2019). Current applications and technological advances are being devised to accommodate this huge data. Evaluation of information and storing are two areas where these tools and methods are used (Kalaian, Kasim, & Kasim, 2019; Anshari, Alas, & Yunus, 2019).

Scholars are starting to take a keen interest in big data. Mikalef, Pappas, Krogstie, and Giannakos (2018) outline the various attempts to describe and describe big data. The academic community has recently shown a great deal of interest in big data (Baig *et al.*, 2021; Rani & Kant, 2020).

Large and complex data sets, known as "big data", necessitate robust methods of storage and analysis. By "big data" we mean extremely huge datasets amassed to discover and study previously unknown relationships between variables.

Big data is necessary because typical data processing software and systems are unable to handle data of this complexity. Big Data technology allows for the collection of massive amounts of data in the form of a database, which can subsequently be used to retrieve patterns among the people or systems studied.

With the use of Big Data, we can gain crucial insight into the data collection process. It is a great improvement over using Excel or some other antiquated program to process data. Text analytics makes it possible for big data and its AI to converge by analyzing all of the data's textual components (Moreno & Redondo, 2016).

The scanned texts are examined based on the categories into which they have been classified and divided. The process of analyzing these writings entails discovering commonalities and tracing the movement of ideas from one to the next. The education sector benefits greatly from big data analytics since it allows for more rapid decision-making and gives institutions a competitive edge through the prompt analysis and application of information.

To further improve student and institution outcomes, several educational institutions are embracing big data analytics for real-time event monitoring and forecasting (Vikas, 2021). Big data analytics also helps schools streamline administrative tasks and boost student participation with timely information. Moreover, big data analytics is employed by a variety of decision-makers to enhance the capacity of educational institutions to make decisions and optimize sales strategies. As a result, the need for data-driven decisions to boost educational quality in the Asia-Pacific region is a major factor propelling the expansion of big data in the education market (Vikas, 2021).

Effective evaluation of huge amounts of data created by educational systems is crucial for fostering appropriate responses to new problems, which in turn improves the quality of learning outcomes (Murumba & Micheni, 2017b).

Since there are several technical challenges associated with big data, such as the need for ongoing upgrades to resources and knowledge, universities and colleges will require substantial funding to address these issues. There are valid privacy concerns, especially about information gathered online. This, together with the digital gap that exists in many countries, creates obstacles to harnessing the potential of big data for the benefit of those who use the educational system.

The use of Big Data (BD) is receiving a lot of attention from top-level executives in many different industries. Despite the abundance of scholarly data (Murumba & Micheni, 2017a), it has not been thoroughly investigated in the education sector. Predicting the circumstances and events that lay the groundwork for a seamless adoption requires the BD theoretical model in the classroom. Therefore, the purpose of this research is to create a model for pinpointing the educational context elements that affect BD. Meanwhile, moderating variables can also have a substantial impact on the proposed model's predictor-BD correlations.

However, in big data research, moderating effects have not been investigated at all. Studies by Asheghi-Oskooeea and Mazloomi (2018) and Baig *et al.* (2021) are just two examples of studies that evaluate the impact of age and size as moderating factors. Therefore, this research aims to construct a theoretical model that accounts for the factors that affect decision-makers' adoption of big data in the educational sector.

1.1. Contributions

This paper reviews the literature and offers recommendations for implementing big data in colleges and universities. For big data to be widely implemented in education, this research can be of assistance to policymakers, managers, and service suppliers. Numerous pedagogical practices have been revolutionized as a result of big data. The capacity to keep tabs on educational institutions is one of the most revolutionary changes brought about by big data. Future educational reform will look very different from current practices. Big data analytics is the study of massive amounts of data using novel techniques and advanced computer programs. Data scientists consider the following three aspects when doing their analyses: Data can be described in terms of their "volume" or total amount; their "velocity" or how quickly they are moved and processed; and their "variety" or different forms and characteristics. Students in higher education should be guided to build abilities in any field through a system that emphasizes the improved quality of results from education. The goals of both students and teachers must be taken into account while designing software for educational purposes. Recognition of facial features and voice-based learning are two examples that, if developed, would revolutionize how quickly students learn. The effective execution of BD systems may coincide with the review's suggested suggestions and repercussions for BD systems professionals and application programmers. Incorporating and endorsing BD activities in one's company is a first step in capitalizing on the benefits of revolutionary technology, and this chapter provides practitioners with a starting point. This chapter also adds to the growing body of scholarship on concepts and models of technological adoption and acceptance, which many scholars have argued should be extended to new contexts.

2. LITERATURE

2.1. Big Data (BD)

Big data is defined as a significant amount of data by Yassine, Singh, Hossain, and Muhammad (2019). In contrast, De Mauro, Greco, and Grimaldi (2016) described it as an asset in the form of information due to its large volume, velocity, and variety. In addition, big data is defined by Zhang (2015) as massive datasets that challenge conventional data processing, management, and analysis techniques. According to Xu and Duan (2019), the three main characteristics of big data are volume, variety, and velocity. Currently, the 3 Cs are expanded into several Vs. Demchenko, Grosso, De Laat, and Membrey (2013), for instance, categorized big data as Volume, Velocity, Variety, Veracity, and Value. Saggi and Jain (2018) classified big data using the same seven characteristics: volume, velocity, variety, valuation, veracity, variability, and value. Insurance and construction (Dresner Advisory Services, 2017), healthcare (Wang, Kung, & Byrd, 2018), telecommunications (Ahmed *et al.*, 2018), and electronic commerce (Wu & Lin, 2018) are just a few of the industries where demand for big data is on the rise. However, this is a problem not exclusive to the education sector and academic world. Oi, Yamada, Okubo, Shimada, and Ogata (2017) note that massive amounts of data are generated in the field of education thanks to the prevalence of online learning environments. Big data has made it possible for educators to track their student's progress in the classroom, analyze their learning styles, and offer immediate feedback (Black & Wiliam, 2018). Students' performance improves as a result of the motivation and contentment brought about by timely and constructive feedback (Zheng & Bender, 2019). Teachers can benefit from analyzing student data to adjust their teaching methods to better meet the requirements of their pupils. Various online learning platforms have been developed, and numerous courses catering to different learning styles have been made available (Holland, 2019). Acquisition and technology are critical to advancing the field of education. Sorensen (2018) argues that large-scale administrative data can be extremely helpful in solving a wide range of academic issues. Therefore, to reduce educational problems, professionals must comprehend the efficacy of big data in education. When it comes to processing and analyzing data sets that are too large or complicated for traditional data processing application software, the field known as "big data" comes into play. Capturing data, storing data, analyzing data, scanning, sharing, uploading, visualizing, querying, updating, privacy, and sourcing data are all problems associated with big data (Cavanillas *et al.*, 2016). Universities store a mountain of information about their students and teachers. Insights gained from analyzing this data will be used to improve the efficiency of educational institutions. Students' activities, test scores, individual progress, and evolving educational requirements would all be central points of attention. Big data allows for the enhancement of data-driven decision-making and organizational, learning, and innovating processes at a variety of levels (Wamba *et al.*, 2017), which, in turn, can generate actionable ideas for delivering long-term value. Desjardins (2019) conducted a study on data volume and found that by 2025, "463 exabytes" of data will be generated daily around the world, and 90% of it will be unstructured. Big data analytics (BD) is a necessary tool for this situation to facilitate quicker decision-making. To uncover information, one can refer to the elaborate procedure of BD analysis. The BD method will leverage cutting-edge analytics tools to alter the BD.

2.2. Adoption of Big Data in the Education Sector

To treat, organize, and extract meaningful information from massive amounts of complicated data, Big Data is a technology instrument that enables its collection and processing. Thus, by combining them, we may produce business intelligence reports (BI or Business Intelligence) that can be used to determine the most pressing educational needs and inform plans to enhance the classroom experience. The field of educational big data (EBD) is experiencing a period of unparalleled acknowledgment of established psychological principles in education, with technologies serving a growing significance in the transformation of traditional methods into digital ones. Because of the scale and significance of data-related issues that need to be addressed in learning behaviors, especially with the deployment of innovative technologies, EBD has emerged as an important area to investigate for both teachers and scholars (Yang & Du, 2016). Big data related to education also helps teachers get ready for their lessons, adapting their methods to better suit their students' requirements. In addition, it lets educators gauge their pupils' levels of enthusiasm and school involvement, as well as the progress they have made in a variety of topic areas and activities (Biswas, 2021). Each student's education can be better-planned thanks to the data acquired by the school using Big Data. The pedagogical practice would benefit from more variety if it utilized many media types for the dissemination of knowledge, such as video, image, audio, and text. Several schools have already begun utilizing Big Data to track and assess student progress, revealing both the challenges they face and the outcomes they achieve. Data helps educators craft a curriculum that is uniquely suited to each student and implement teaching strategies that are effective for their subject area (Biswas, 2021). With the use of big data analytics, educational institutions have been able to advance educational goals and boost students' ability to study. Students' success should be measured by more than just how they do on standard tests and exams. Big data analytics makes it possible to keep tabs on each student and gain insight into their areas of strength and improvement, as well as their response times and the types of problems they struggle with. Teachers and mentors can help students develop their potential by providing access to relevant resources and providing individualized guidance to those who need it. There is a lot of information generated by online education activities like courses and lessons. Teachers can better support their student's academic growth by tracking their progress, providing immediate feedback, and identifying trends in student performance.

2.3. Factors for Adopting BD in the Education Sector

The success of businesses and individuals depends on their willingness to adopt new technologies. The technology adoption model (TAM) (Davis, 1985) and the theory of planned behavior (TPB) (Ajzen, 1991) are just two of the many models of technology acceptance that have been created and evaluated. However, the UTAUT model (Venkatesh *et al.*, 2003) stands out as the most thorough option. The purpose of this model is to examine the spread and acceptance of new technologies by combining existing models and theories. The TAM (Davis, 1985), TAM2 (Venkatesh & Davis, 2000), TAM3 (Venkatesh & Bala, 2008), and the UTAUT model have all been utilized in previous studies of BD adoption in businesses (Brünink, 2016; Rahman, 2016; Demoulin & Coussement, 2018; Verma *et al.*, 2018). Since their initial implementation, acceptance models have undergone numerous revisions and even morphed into entirely new models. Because the UTAUT model is already well-developed, we enrich it by adding two new variables (found to be relevant in this study) that explain why some businesses choose to embrace BD while others do not. Behavioral intention to use is a latent variable that is determined by the TAM's two constructs, 'perceived usefulness' (PU) and 'perceived ease of use' (PEOU), which are impacted by independent variables. The Technology, Organization, and Environment (TOE) Framework was first presented by Tornatzky and Fleischer (1990). Adoption, according to TEO, is driven by technological, organizational, and environmental variables.

2.4. Perceived Usefulness

People's expectations about how a piece of technology would affect their work are known as their "perceived usefulness" (PU) and their "perceived ease of use" (PEOU) (Davis, 1989). The model defines "ease of use" as the extent to which external auditors expect no mental or physical strain from utilizing big data analytics solutions. Job relevance, outcome demonstrability, image, complexity, management support, social presence, attitude, anxiety, accessibility, perceived enjoyment, facilitating conditions, self-efficacy, and end-user support are all examples of external variables used to measure perceived usefulness (PU) (Lee *et al.*, 2003). According to Venkatesh *et al.* (2003), "the degree of ease associated with the use of the tool" (Venkatesh *et al.*, 2003, p. 26) is a good definition of effort expectation, which they found to be similar to the meaning and influence of perceived ease of use. Once again, Janvrin *et al.* (2008) offer backing for this idea. Therefore, it is anticipated that the adoption of big data analytics systems will increase when external auditors find them to be user-friendly.

2.5. Perceived Ease of Use (PEOU)

Attitude, nervousness, usability, availability, spontaneity, perceived pleasure, enabling conditions, self-worth, social factors (*i.e.*, subjective norm, social pressure), and managerial support are some of the external variables that have been examined for the concept of perceived simplicity of use (PEOU) (Lee *et al.*, 2003). Anchoring (*i.e.*, computer self-efficacy), external control (*i.e.*, facilitating conditions), emotion (*i.e.*, computer anxiety), and adjustments-based theoretical model (*i.e.*, perceived enjoyment and objective usability) are the primary determinants of PEOU (Venkatesh, 2000). Another factor that may affect how beneficial something is thought to be is how simple it is to use. When external auditors have a favorable impression of big data analytics tools, for example, they are more likely to make use of them, which should lead to enhanced performance.

• **Observability**

One of the five properties of innovations in the Diffusion of Innovations (DOI) hypothesis is observability (Rogers, 2003). This quality makes it simple to see the results of technology and share your findings with others. Brown-Liburd *et al.* (2015) note that the proliferation of data can overwhelm decision-makers with data that exceeds their capacity to process. Leavitt (2013) notes, however, that while big data does increase corporate value, it is too complicated and pricey for most small enterprises.

• **Trialability**

It is the D.O.I. theory that is responsible for the trialability element (Rogers, 2003). Trial runs of innovations should cost little to nothing to be successful (Fichman & Kemerer, 1993). Previous studies (such as Arts *et al.*, 2011) have confirmed the importance of this variable. Trialability is linked to the possibility of having no positive effect or value. "Adopters look unfavorably on innovations that are difficult to put through a trial period or whose benefits are difficult to see or describe" (Fichman and Kemerer, 1993). These aspects cast doubt on the actual worth of the idea.

- **Complexity**

The DOI theory is also the source of the complexity consideration (Rogers, 2003). The volume, velocity, variety, authenticity, and significance of big data make it a very vast and intricate data set. However, large organizations with access to experts and highly qualified engineers may find the process of integrating big data technology into their operations to be considerably less daunting. The speed at which big data is generated calls for complicated analysis in real-time and the extraction of complex patterns (Chardonnens *et al.*, 2013; Najafabadi *et al.*, 2015). Data complexity, computational complexity, and system complexity are all discussed by Jin *et al.* (2015) as obstacles to big data processing. The difficulties of large data integration are reported by Russom (2013). According to Amudhavel *et al.* (2015), typical data processing applications are unable to deal with the scale or complexity of big data. Big data's complexity is defined as its inaccessibility and difficulty of use (Verma, 2017). There have been experiments with complexity in a variety of academic settings. Complexity has been found to have a deleterious effect on the uptake of innovation in education. However, users' perceptions of complexity may vary. There is a correlation between moderator size and complexity and technological adoption. Evidence suggests that larger organizations are better able to spread innovations.

- **Overall Expenditure of Ownership**

To be cost-effective, technology must not have any major hidden costs during its existence and be simple to dispose of once its usefulness has ended. Nearly all big data tools are free and open-source. It would be interesting to observe how much the total cost of ownership increases if vendor support is required. Thus, we incorporate this aspect into the qualitative analysis of this research.

- **Financial Resource**

The term "financial resource" was used to refer to the available funds for implementing cutting-edge technological solutions and for recruiting prospective office personnel. According to research (Yadegaridehkordi *et al.*, 2020), this factor significantly differentiates early adopters from late adopters. Adoption and financial resources appear to moderate the effect of size. This research confirmed that BDA is positively affected by financial resources. Previous research has corroborated these findings. The correlation between institutional funding and BDA is strong, regardless of the size of the institution. Since then, institutions' budgets have been separated from their staff sizes.

• Technological Factors

In terms of the company's seen benefits and the capacity of the technology to integrate with current systems, technological aspects characterize the technology's perceived features. Technological preparedness, also known as technology competence (Huda *et al.*, 2017), is a hypothesis used to evaluate an organization's preparedness to adopt big data technologies. Understanding has been greatly aided by the identification and use of various technology use cases for big data as an integral part of the ionization advances (Izhar & Shoid, 2016).

The institution needs to learn how easy it is to use the big data solution, how well it integrates with current infrastructure, and what advantages it may offer (Sam & Chatwin, 2019). Marketers can benefit from the IT setting by increasing their reliance on digital developments and adopting novel approaches to problem-solving and choice-making (Elgendy & Elragal, 2016).

The advent of new technologies such as computers, smartphones, tablets, sensors, social media, audio, video, spatial and geo-location data, machines, the internet of things, clickstream data, user-generated content, commercial transactions, and so on has allowed businesses to generate massive amounts of data. Therefore, data becomes difficult to manage using current tools, and new approaches to data storage and analysis are required if we are to extract value from it. It is crucial to conduct a reliability study on Big Data. Through testing and analysis, reliability technology raises product dependability. Information of many kinds can be gathered with the help of social media. Several challenges exist in making use of social media data, such as the abundance of noise and the uncertainty of where the data originated. In this context, companies employ social media platforms like Twitter, Facebook, Instagram, Telegram, WhatsApp, and Google+ as powerful marketing channels for information discovery, analysis, and distribution.

It can also help ensure that no defective goods are made. Big Data takes in massive amounts of data and analyzes it to provide high-quality results quickly. Only when all the data is searchable and well-described can reliability technology engineers conduct system-wide reliability studies (Williamson, 2018). The term "technology infrastructure" refers to the physical components of a company's or university's network. To implement technological breakthroughs, institutions require several resources, such as the physical assets mentioned above. The crucial project of moving forward with digital universities is carried out by the technology infrastructure, which also reforms higher education and constructs a covert marketing system in higher education. Outsourcing firms from the commercial sector, software developers, cloud hosting companies, data analytics designers, and a whole host of other technical specialists are needed to build higher education's IT infrastructure (Williamson, 2018). Higher education's huge data can be made more complex by technological infrastructure.

• Fault Tolerance

The fault tolerance metric is gleaned from academic studies on large data. No known empirical research on technology adoption made use of this variable. Hadoop, a system for processing large amounts of data, is notable for its resilience in the face of failure. High throughputs and fault tolerance are provided by Hadoop's usage of commodity hardware (Abouzeid *et al.*, 2009). To ensure that data is always accessible, it stores several replicas of it among the cluster's nodes (Nemschoff, 2013). When compared to traditional database systems, Hadoop offers this distinct benefit.

• Flexibility

The literature we have so far implies that IT infrastructure adaptability is a crucial competence (Byrd & Turner, 2000). The adaptability of a system or technology determines how well it will be received by its target audience (Basoglu *et al.*, 2007; Seneler *et al.*, 2008). Data can be gathered from a wider variety of sources with the use of big data tools and technology (Rahman & Rutz, 2015). Business analysts Abouzeid *et al.* (2009) stress the importance of a flexible query interface for managing analytical data.

• Relative Advantage

According to Rogers's (2003) key work, "The Diffusion of Innovation," relative advantage is one of the top five features of innovations that affect the pace of adoption. One of the top three innovation features is a relative advantage, according to previous meta-analysis studies on the adoption of technological innovation (Ramamurthy *et al.*, 2008). "The extent to which a new technology or invention is thought to be more useful than its predecessor," according to the dictionary definition of relative advantage. The notion of RA is compared to that of TAM's perceived usefulness and to that of UTAUT's concept of performance expectancy. Several researchers have made extensive use of RA. Students are more inclined to embrace M-learning if they see its value. The RA of the e-learning environment develops as a result of mobile phones' distinct advantages over more conventional forms of education. Learners appreciate M-learning because it allows them to utilize a device of their choosing, process information efficiently regardless of time or place, and can be accessed virtually anywhere with an internet connection.

• **Personal Creativity and Innovation (PI)**

Personal innovation (PI) in the field of information technology refers to an individual's propensity to experiment with and adopt new IT regardless of the stated experience of others. When compared to others who are less creative, innovative people have an easier time grasping the practicality and use of emerging technologies. It has been observed that those who are very innovative are also highly receptive to technological advancements. An innovative person is willing to try new things and is comfortable with the unknown. Similar to the social norm in TRA, TAM2, and TPB and image in IDT, social influence (SI) is described as "a person's perception that most people who are imported to him think he should or should not perform the behavior in question" (Ajzen, 1991). In other words, social influence (SI) refers to the influence that people's social networks, including their friends, family, and coworkers, have on their decision to take part in a certain activity. Because of theoretical and measurement difficulties, Davis (1989) left the SI to construct out of the first TAM; however, it was included in TAM2 because of its importance in understanding the external influence of others on an individual's behavior. Numerous practical studies in the field of information systems (*e.g.*, Venkatesh *et al.*, 2003) have shown SI as a necessary precondition for BI.

• **Performance Expectancy**

To put it another way, performance expectancy is "the degree to which an individual believes that using the system will help him or her to attain gains in job performance" (Venkatesh *et al.*, 2003). How confident people are that increased productivity will result from technology use. The perceived value of technology is synonymous with this concept. Users' expectations of software technology's usability, infrastructure performance in terms of runtime, and computing resource usage all contribute to the performance expectancy factor. In his model (UTAUT), Venkatesh (2000) includes this variable as an independent one. Information technology (IT) personnel strive for professional growth and advancement (Venkatesh & Zhang, 2010; Zhang, 2017). Performance expectancy is grounded in concepts from the Technology Acceptance Model (TAM), TAM2, the Combined TAM and the Theory of Planned Behavior (CTAMTPB), the Motivational Model (MM), the model of PC usage (MPCU), the Innovation Diffusion Theory (IDT), and the Social Cognitive Theory (SCT) (*i.e.* perceived usefulness, extrinsic motivation, job-fit, relative advantage, and outcome expectancy). According to multiple studies (Zhou, Lu, & Wang, 2010; Venkatesh, Thong, & Xu, 2016), this factor is the most important predictor of future behavior in both voluntary and mandated circumstances.

- **Scalability**

One of the most crucial features of a successful data warehouse operation is the ability to scale (Rahman & Rutz, 2015; Sen & Jacob, 1998; Sen & Sinha, 2005). Anagnostopoulos and Triantafillou (2020), Menon and Sarkar (2016), and Tsai *et al.* (2015) all point to scalability as a key component of effective data analytics in the realm of big data. Most conventional relational databases are not scalable to handle data volumes of several hundred terabytes. According to big data research papers (Shvachko, 2011), Hadoop's scalability is a major factor in the framework's widespread use.

- **Compatibility**

Compatibility refers to how well new technology fits in with the values, knowledge, and requirements of its potential consumers (Majeed *et al.*, 2022). One of the most important factors in BD prediction is compatibility. The compatibility on BD can be adjusted by age. Age has been shown to play a mediating role in several adoption settings. The compatibility criterion was first proposed in Rogers' (2003a) DOI theory. It is one of the five pillars of innovation. Traditional data storage systems, transformation tools, and reporting tools are incompatible with big data and its tools and technology. This is because big data is typically unstructured, voluminous, and fast-moving. This is why developers need to learn new skills to make effective use of big data tools and technologies (Lee, 2017). Normal data, as opposed to structured data, is what traditional tools, technology, and skill sets have been built upon. Compatibility refers to how well a new technology fits in with the values, knowledge, and requirements of its potential users. Consistent research has shown that compatibility is a major indicator of BDA. The compatibility on BD can be adjusted by age. Age has been shown to play a mediating role in several adoption settings.

- **Reliability**

The dependability of technological systems is seen as fundamental and crucial (Barlow, 1984). According to the technology adoption taxonomy (Seneler *et al.*, 2008), this is a crucial component. Hundreds of terabytes to petabytes of data can be safely stored in the Hadoop Distributed File System (HDFS) (Shvachko *et al.*, 2010). There is no downtime in Hadoop's distributed file system. In the event of a node failure, the remaining nodes take control. Three copies of the data are sent to different nodes. There is consequently far less risk of losing data.

- **Confidentiality and Safety**

According to multiple studies (Jain *et al.*, 2016; Raguseo, 2018; Sun *et al.*, 2018; Wessel & Helmer, 2020; Wu *et al.*, 2017), data privacy is a major hurdle for big data adoption. Existing research implies that there are certain needs that big data technologies must meet, such as the ability to handle sensitive data about persons, businesses, and governments (Lee, 2017; Menon & Sarkar, 2016). Since much data comes from users' personal data, privacy, secrecy, and identification must be ensured by big data technology, as stated by Richards and King (2014). According to Gray (2014), Hadoop lacks the necessary security features for secure enterprise data deployment. The capacity to pinpoint the precise location of a mobile phone user is a key feature of modern mobile communication systems. Many people think that location-based apps and services have a lot of promise for making money, thanks to the accessibility provided by mobile technology. Since service providers will know the user's precise location and possibly even their travel pattern, this capability may provide more personalized service (*i.e.*, service providers can provide information services like advertising and navigation based on the user's location), but it also poses potential privacy problems. Personal safety and moral principles are at the heart of security and privacy concerns. BDA is impeded by privacy and security worries [35]. Previous studies in the field of education found an inverse relationship between technology and privacy and security. When it comes to worries about personal safety and BD, one moderating factor is age.

2.6. Perceived Credibility (PC)

Perceived credibility (PC) in this study refers to how well students believe their financial and personal information is protected from unauthorized access. Perceived believability is a crucial sign of behavioral intention to utilize an IS, as stated by Hanudin (2007). Two main factors contribute to how credible something is: security and privacy. Privacy refers to the safeguarding of various types of data that are acquired (with or without the knowledge of the users) during the users' interactions with the internet, while security refers to the safeguarding of information or systems against unauthorized intrusions or outflows (Hoffman *et al.*, 1999).

- **Trust**

One of the most crucial aspects of e-commerce and marketing research is students' trust. In other words, having faith in the site you are buying from is crucial. The concept of perceived risk had been proposed in earlier research. Indeed, there is a robust correlation between worry and confidence. Earlier ideas of IT adoption centered on people's propensity to embrace the technology being adopted. But their "trust" in the technology also reflects their confidence in it. The concept of "utility" is reflective of people's trust in technology in a roundabout way. User acceptability in the context of e-learning encompasses not just technological acceptance but also the approval of m-commerce service providers. This highlights the importance of trust in gaining user acceptance. The success of mobile commerce depends on gaining students' trust. Trust must be incorporated into studies of mobile commerce, with a focus on consumers' confidence in m-commerce service providers. Concepts like usefulness and usability need to incorporate trust. The topic of students' faith in educational institutions and service providers is ripe with literature and theory.

- **Economic Efficiency/Cost-Effectiveness**

If one utilizes an IS for work purposes, his or her employer will be responsible for covering the cost of the IS. Wired Internet-based information systems have cheap operating costs. However, many wireless customers still have to cover the hefty costs associated with making a wireless transaction. Therefore, it is important to think about price when it comes to e-commerce. Economists argue that new technologies lead to price increases but also provide benefits (Kohli *et al.*, 2012). The majority of the big data tools and technologies based on Hadoop are free because they are developed as open-source projects. Case studies have shown that big data applications have helped save money for businesses. According to Bologa *et al.* (2010), the availability of large datasets has facilitated the timely identification of insurance fraud. Timeliness of response using big data, according to Villars *et al.* (2011), helped get rid of legal and financial expenditures related to fund recovery.

2.7. Environmental Factors

Market conditions, legal mandates, and societal and cultural standards are all examples of elements that make up an organization's environment. The dynamism of the sector, the presence of competitors, the presence of trading partners, and the presence of authorities are all examples of environmental influences. Tornatzky and Fleischer's (1990) Theory of the Entrepreneurial Environment (TOE) framework includes an environmental context that reflects the external aspects of the business environment that explain the innovation's adoption. It argues that an entrepreneur's choice to accept new technologies depends on the context in which they operate. That is, there are specific permutations of environmental factors that tend to go hand-in-hand with technological adoption. To be sure, dependent-partner preparedness has been analyzed as a construct of the environmental setting in TOE research.

2.8. Organizational Factors

Organizational factors include things like the size of the business, its financial and human resources, internal structure, goal for the future, and outlook. Technology's scale, structure, culture, and availability all play a role in the organizational setting in which it is deployed. New technology adoption and upkeep may be affected by the size of an organization's IT team (Sun *et al.*, 2018). As new capabilities in data management, big data tools and technologies necessitate a workforce and other resources to train and maintain. One of the organizational determinants of implementing data warehousing technology is the size of the organization, as identified by Ramamurthy *et al.* (2008). Top management support for technology adoption is especially important for small and medium-sized businesses. Executive support and permission for Big Data in higher education can be strengthened with the help of the top management (Sun *et al.*, 2018). Furthermore, top-level management's participation in big data implementation and use is crucial for gaining buy-in and sponsorship for the technology and for removing obstacles to its adoption. The opportunities for creating eco-friendly products that appeal to a worldwide clientele are vastly expanded by BD. Predictive analytics in the field can be used to foresee how well a green product would function. The optimum marketing and operations plans can be determined and supply chain expenses can be managed with the help of accurate forecasting. By using Big Data Analytical, businesses may anticipate market shifts and act strategically, giving them a leg up on the competition. Previous research (Chong & Olesen, 2017) indicated that backing from upper management improves the likelihood of an organization embracing big data. Support and sponsorship of new technology, as well as assistance in overcoming change barriers, can be greatly aided by the participation of top management in the deployment and usage of Big Data. One of the organizational elements for data warehouse effectiveness is believed to be organizational commitment (Ramamurthy *et al.*, 2008). Management endorsement is essential for successful big data implementation (Russom, 2013). IT departments and data scientists need to lead the charge in demonstrating the ROI of big data initiatives to win over upper management (Rajpurohit, 2013).

- **Functionality**

When a piece of technology has good functionality, its properties and features match the needs of its intended end user. Functionality in the big data arena refers to the capacity of big data tools and technologies to process massive amounts of data, the vast majority of which is unstructured and hence inaccessible to traditional data storage systems and their accompanying tools and technologies.

The TAM field has not considered this variable. In our qualitative analysis, this is taken into account.

• Effort Expectation

This aspect is taken from Venkatesh *et al.*'s (2003, 2012) UTAUT technology acceptance model. A person's perception of the amount of effort required to utilize a piece of technology is "related to the degree of ease associated with the use of technology" (Venkatesh *et al.*, 2003). With the unstructured nature of big data comes complexity; therefore, it will be fascinating to observe how user-friendly the big data tools are.

• Facilitating Conditions

To what extent do people perceive that the organizational and technical infrastructure exists to facilitate the usage of the system? This is what is meant by "facilitating conditions" (Venkatesh *et al.*, 2003). According to the literature, user confidence in the system is measured by "the degree to which an individual believes that an organizational and technical infrastructure exists to support the use of the system" (Venkatesh *et al.*, 2003, p. 453). IB services necessitate a certain set of competencies, assets, and technical infrastructure, and the majority of the time, the client is responsible for covering these costs (Zhou *et al.*, 2010). The enabling conditions component was originally conceived as part of the UTAUT model for technology acceptance created by Venkatesh *et al.* One of the most important considerations in deciding on a data warehouse architecture is the availability of necessary resources (Ariyachandra & Watson, 2010; Rahman, 2017). This is one of the technology adoption taxonomy elements identified by Seneler *et al.* (2008). Given the complexity of big data technologies, we hypothesize that their widespread adoption is driven by favorable circumstances. There may be external environment conditions (like vendor support) that help. Internally, enabling conditions, such as IT infrastructure support, may also be required.

• Subjective Norms

The theory of reasoned action (TRA) proposed by Fishbein and Ajzen (1975) is the source of the subjective norms/social influence element. Ajzen (1991) later incorporated it into his theory of planned behavior (TPB). A person's subjective norms or social influence refers to his belief that the majority of his significant others think he should or should not engage in certain conduct.

- **Social Influence**

When it comes to mandatory technology use, societal pressure becomes very important (Venkatesh *et al.*, 2003). In a necessary setting, people may adopt a new piece of technology out of necessity rather than choice. This could account for the mixed results found in additional studies attempting to validate the model (Chauhan & Jaiswal, 2016).

- **Self-Efficacy**

Self-efficacy is defined as "the sense that one can accomplish a goal" (Lee *et al.*, 2003). This aspect of the technology acceptance model was first proposed by Igbaria *et al.* (1995) to analyze an individual's confidence in their ability to perform various tasks on a computer. According to Sun *et al.* (2016), the user's level of awareness is also an important consideration when deciding to accept a new piece of technology. The authors argue that cautious adopters will have a greater chance of seeing technology favorably.

3. BENEFITS OF BIG DATA IN THE EDUCATION SECTOR

- **Academic Productivity**

Big data is used by educators to study students' performance and uncover openings for deeper engagement. They may improve the educational program by, for instance, analyzing things like dropout rates, overall enrolment, and pupil success rates (Bahrynovska, 2022).

- **Teaching Efficiency**

The data collected can then be used by educators to improve classroom conditions and conduct more accurate evaluations of course effectiveness. Errors on quizzes, wrong answers, and how long students take to finish tasks are just some of the areas where analytics might shed light (Bahrynovska, 2022). This gives educators the flexibility to make last-minute course corrections and boost short-term performance.

- **Organization of Processes**

Prospective students' internet, social media, and mobile device movements can all be monitored with the aid of customer relationship management software. "Cookies" allow for the retargeting of advertisements to prospective students after they have visited the college's online resource (Bahrynovska, 2022). This has the potential to enhance enrollment and, by extension, revenue.

- **Development within the Institute (In-house Progress)**

The campus's monetary and commercial operations benefit from technology's efficiency and productivity as well. Network log analysis, for instance, can drastically cut down on support response times (Bahrynovska, 2022). The improved academic performance of the student body has a multiplicative effect on the school's reputation.

- **Map Student Learning**

Teachers can evaluate their student's progress in class using Big Data system technologies (Biswas, 2021). Planning educational procedures that can satisfy students' requirements is greatly aided by the ability to share and analyze data in some systems. Analysis of individual student performance also makes it possible to tailor instruction to the needs of each learner. Therefore, it is easier for educators to comprehend the constraints and resources and, with this knowledge, to devise strategies to overcome the obstacles.

- **Distributed Requests**

Through the use of distributed queries, the gathered information can be retrieved. Instead of using separate database shards, this can be accomplished with the help of big data technologies using simultaneous searches.

- **Freedom of Tech Stack/Tech Stack Independence**

As for the data processing tools, they might be anything from software to hardware. With the use of Big Data, we can analyze the data from thousands of classrooms and classroom teachers to determine the most successful teaching methods and determine the best learning environments.

- **Reduce the Potential for Student Dropout**

The number of students who will eventually abandon their course of study can be estimated with the help of big data. Using big data analytics, schools may look at a student's performance throughout the year and determine if they are at risk of failing out of school. Institutions of higher learning might also gauge potential interest in a new course offering by surveying current students. Reduction in school failure and dropout rates is observed, particularly in countries with an economy still emerging. Dropout and failure rates have been shown to significantly decrease in schools that include Big Data in their administrative routine (Biswas, 2021). Using the platform's analysis, the administration may predict which children will drop out of school or receive failing grades based on their attendance and dismissal patterns. This can be quantified through the student's actions on the learning management system, such as attendance and performance in class (Biswas, 2021). By identifying the pattern of behavior in advance, the educational staff can intervene and provide solutions before the student gives up.

- **Manage the Business's Finances and Operations**

Because of their versatility, the methods of analyzing large amounts of data are great partners of school administration. One of these concerns is the administration of the school's funds and other resources. Cash flow characteristics like retention and default rates can be monitored with the help of technology (Biswas, 2021). Big Data's reliance on metrics means that the tool can accurately predict the outcomes for the educational institution, which can make changes gradually to protect against big losses or to allow for the prediction of investments in certain industries. Because of this, it must be kept in mind that Big Data can revolutionize and make management evolve when applied to education.

- **Maintaining Open and Honest Communication**

Data from any section of the database is made available to anyone involved in the educational process, even if that data is being used for something else at the time. The analyst should disregard the constraints of the data's physical location if access has been granted. Built-in tools handle data delivery mechanically (Bahrynovska, 2022).

- **Multiplication of Data**

The ease with which data can be moved between databases facilitates the joining of previously separate systems. Modern technology has made it possible to design elaborate buildings that can be accessed in a dependable and hassle-free manner.

- **Accelerate the Instructional Process**

When big data analytics are used in the classroom, students have access to a wealth of new resources that can help them expand their horizons and develop their abilities. Teachers are better able to help students overcome obstacles to learning when they have access to relevant data that allows them to enhance the quality of the reading material they deliver. In addition, students benefit from big data analytics since they may take advantage of individualized courses that are tailored to their specific needs. It is hoped that the increased focus on the material that is most relevant to each student would arise from the use of these individualized modules.

- **Personalization**

Big data technology typically serves as a classroom platform, allowing students to participate in lectures and complete assigned tasks. The system is optimized to check for correct and incorrect answers during practice, pinpointing where the training is lacking (Biswas, 2021). Therefore, the platform may utilize the acquired data to forecast each student's success, allowing for enhanced and individualized education. This provides the teacher with a more solid foundation on which to base the definition of their educational practice and the close monitoring of the class's progress. Better content and format indicators that correspond to the student's life can still be provided.

4. THE FUTURE OF BIG DATA IN EDUCATION

As technology makes it easier to spot at-risk individuals early on, class sizes in universities should shrink as a result. Teachers will also benefit from the program because it will reveal which specific areas of expertise children lack. The technology will also aid high school seniors in selecting a college. In the future, students will not even need to apply to the universities they want to attend; robots will pick them for them. A digital portfolio will be provided to each graduate to aid them in their job search and aid businesses in making informed decisions when hiring specialists. The focus shifts from the teacher to the individual learner. The concept of how learning experiences are structured is evolving as a result of instructional intelligence built on big data. In addition to digitizing texts, they can also be converted into numerical data for use in the classroom. Such analytics will lead to a shift in the material itself, making for a more fluid user experience. There is an increase in the number of "smart" applications and courses. The courses themselves will likely evolve; perhaps they will even become meta-subjects. The use of novel techniques like forecasting (where a set of known data may be used to anticipate an unknown of interest), network analysis, structure determination, and clustering will become standard practice in the field of educational analytics. The curriculum may be tailored to each student, and teachers can make better use of limited resources thanks to new methods of tracking and assessing both the teaching process and the student's progress.

5. IMPLICATIONS

Given Big Data's early uptake and novelty, many prior studies have focused solely on its benefits, risks, and potential. Many researchers have examined BD, with the most recent works emphasizing one perspective or singling out TAM and UTAUT theory for special attention. This study is the first to propose a model fusing UTAUT and TAM theories as a potential predictor of deliberate intents to use

BD. Because of this, there are fresh insights to be gleaned from the convergence and implementation of all various BD adoption approaches.

This chapter provides useful information and advances a viable paradigm for future studies of BD. When introducing novel technology, it is crucial to take into account users' perspectives. This study proposes a model built on TEO, UTAUT, and TAM to investigate the factors that motivate college students in low-income countries like Palestine to adopt mobile learning. In order to determine what factors influence students' plans to use M-learning in the future, a study model has been developed. This study's findings provide crucial empirical evidence for the field of M-learning, particularly because they come from a least developed country. The findings of this empirical study may also be useful to administrators and policymakers who are considering implementing M-learning in settings similar to the one studied here.

Existing public agencies can learn about their own BD capabilities using the information in this chapter, which focuses on activities with targeted outcomes, organizational dynamics, resources, skills, and possible services. Within their departments, government organizations can pinpoint the most widespread roadblocks to building and executing an efficient BD and devise strategies to overcome them. The research has also contributed in several useful ways. With the successful implementation of BD systems, the author recommends several important recommendations and repercussions for BD systems practitioners and application developers. It is essential to link the features and capabilities of the BD system to the tasks that need to be completed. The same holds for the expected performance of the system.

By taking this approach, practitioners might expect better results from BD system implementations. This study provides practitioners with a starting point for adopting and endorsing BD activities within their organization to maximize the benefits of revolutionary technology, especially for government organizations.

Businesses must develop new competencies to successfully adopt, implement, and manage BD. Data scientists, for example, are in high demand because their unique skill set combines engineering, statistics, and a solid understanding of business. Employees with these abilities are invaluable to businesses because they assist them in mining data created by the company and its consumers. This shifts the focus from the CEO's intuition to hard evidence, altering the decision-making process. Questions concerning the data, processing difficulties, and data management concerns all occur during the "data cycle of life" and must be addressed by educational institutions adopting BD. The data itself raises questions about its size, variety, speed, accuracy, volatility, value, and presentation.

Acquiring data, storing it in databases, cleaning and manipulating it, selecting the right model, and presenting the results are all examples of data processing jobs. Last but not least, ethical factors like user privacy and security are essential to effective data management.

CONCLUSION

In this study, we reviewed the literature on how big data is being used in universities and colleges and what factors are driving this trend. Understanding how to collect the knowledge to develop its reliability in educational settings is a major obstacle to the widespread adoption of big data in research at higher education institutions. Adopting a framework that works with the current higher education institution and putting it to use is one way to incorporate big data into the educational process and uncover solutions to pressing problems in the field of HEIs. In recent years, big data has emerged as a crucial tool in the classroom. As such, this research aims to dissect the various motivations for, barriers to, and varieties of big data (BD) implementation within the academic setting.

The Big Data procedure needs to work with the current framework of the academic world. Providers of big data services have a responsibility to ensure that any necessary technological upgrades are backward compatible with their clients' current infrastructure. Providers of big data services also have a responsibility to ensure that the newest software is compatible with the most commonly used operating systems. Developing or recruiting responsible management is a crucial part of business development. This highlights the need for competent managers who understand the bigger picture of BD. Top-level management is responsible for devising plans and strategies, keeping an eye on the nuts and bolts, meeting deadlines, and solving any problems that may arise. Managers' roles in BD need to be defined explicitly to ensure success. The policies of the government should be adaptable and make it simple for the higher education sector to acquire information. To secure users' private and sensitive information, institutions should clearly state what data is publicly available and adhere to government guidance. BD relies heavily on available funding. Consequently, organizations should set aside the necessary cash for BD. When deciding to implement a new technology, there are many paths to take into account. However, given the limited resources at hand, we must establish priorities and settle on the most essential and cost-effective solutions. The use of BD eventually enhances the entire arrangement while decreasing costs over time. To run BD infrastructure, the higher education industry needs qualified and skilled personnel. After an institution has adopted a big data solution, the vendor of that solution must give training for the institution's staff to manage the setup. In addition, organizations can fill permanent positions with trained employees or temporary positions with contractors.

To improve the current setup and remain competitive, the higher education sector should periodically evaluate the usage of technology to determine if additional or upgraded technology is required. Keeping the pressure on the opposition requires the correct adoption of big data. Privacy and security issues institutions have the means to safeguard big data from outside interference. Standardized and proper passwords help secure access to the data. As a result, strong passwords need to have multiple components.

Pre-boot password setting is an option. The safeguards should prevent hackers and spies from gaining access to the data. The user should not be able to see everything in the system. For restricted access, username and password requirements must be set up. The potential for data misuse necessitates regulatory requirements imposed by institutions. Intruders do not need remote access to the data to cause problems. Instead of having the data spread across several hard drives, it should be stored safely on a few central servers. It is important to verify the network's risk assessment.

REFERENCES

Ahmed, E., Yaqoob, I., Hashem, I.A.T., Shuja, J., Imran, M., Guizani, N., Bakhsh, S.T. (2018). *Recent advances and challenges in mobile big data. IEEE Communications Magazine, 56(2), 102–108.*. China: East China Normal University.
[http://dx.doi.org/10.1109/MCOM.2018.1700294]

Ajzen, I. (1991). The theory of planned behavior. *Organ. Behav. Hum. Decis. Process., 50*(2), 179-211.
[http://dx.doi.org/10.1016/0749-5978(91)90020-T]

Asheghi-Oskooeea, H., Mazloomi, N. (2018). A strategic entrepreneurship model based on corporate governance in the Iranian manufacturing enterprises. *Int. J. Econ. Manag. Account., 26*, 25-56.

Anshari, M., Alas, Y., Yunus, N. (2016). A survey study of smartphones behavior in Brunei: A proposal of Modelling big data strategies*International Journal of Cyber Behavior, 6*(4), 60-72.

Baig, M.I., Shuib, L., Yadegaridehkordi, E. (2021). A Model for Decision-Makers' Adoption of Big Data in the Education Sector. *Sustainability (Basel), 13*(24), 13995.
[http://dx.doi.org/10.3390/su132413995]

Brünink, L. (2016). *Cross-functional Big Data integration: Applying the UTAUT model.*. The Netherlands: University of Twente.

Biswas, S. (2021). Big Data in education: what are the advantages and how to adopt? Available from: https://www.linkedin.com/pulse/big-data-education-what-advantages-how-adopt-sudhin-biswas?trk=read_related_article-card_title

Black, P., Wiliam, D. (2018). Classroom assessment and pedagogy. *Asess. Educ., 25*(6), 551-575.
[http://dx.doi.org/10.1080/0969594X.2018.1441807]

Cavanillas, J.M., Curry, E., Wahlster, W. (2016). *New Horizons for a Data-Driven Economy: A Roadmap for Usage and Exploitation of Big Data in Europe.* Springer.
[http://dx.doi.org/10.1007/978-3-319-21569-3]

Chong, J.L.L., Olesen, K. (2017). A technology-organization-environment perspective on ecoeffectiveness: A meta-analysis. *AJIS Australas. J. Inf. Syst., 21*, 1-26.
[http://dx.doi.org/10.3127/ajis.v21i0.1441]

Davis, F. (1985). A technology acceptance model for empirically testing new end-user information systems.

Thesis: Massachusetts Institute of Technology, Sloan School of Management.

Demoulin, N.T.M., Coussement, K. (2020). Acceptance of text-mining systems: The signaling role of information quality. *Inf. Manage., 57*(1), 103120.
[http://dx.doi.org/10.1016/j.im.2018.10.006]

Desjardins, J. (2019). How much data is generated each day? Available from: https://www.weforum.org/agenda/2019/04/how-much-data-is-generated-each-day-cf4bddf29f/

De Mauro, A., Greco, M., Grimaldi, M. (2016). A formal definition of Big Data based on its essential features. *Libr. Rev., 65*(3), 122-135.
[http://dx.doi.org/10.1108/LR-06-2015-0061]

Demchenko, Y., Grosso, P., De Laat, C., Membrey, P. (2013). Addressing big data issues in scientific data infrastructure. *International Conference on Collaboration Technologies and Systems (CTS),* San Diego, CA, USA48-55.
[http://dx.doi.org/10.1109/CTS.2013.6567203]

Dresner Advisory Services. (2017). Big data adoption: State of the market. Available from: https://www.zoomdata. com/master-class/state-market/big-data-adoption

Elgendy, N., Elragal, A. (2016). Big data analytics in support of the decision making process. *Procedia Comput. Sci., 100*, 1071-1084.
[http://dx.doi.org/10.1016/j.procs.2016.09.251]

Holland, A.A. (2019). Effective principles of informal online learning design: A theory-building metasynthesis of qualitative research. *Comput. Educ., 128*, 214-226.
[http://dx.doi.org/10.1016/j.compedu.2018.09.026]

Huda, M., Maseleno, A., Shahrill, M., Jasmi, K.A., Mustari, I., Basiron, B. (2017). Exploring adaptive teaching competencies in big data era. *Int. J. Emerg. Technol. Learn., 12*(3), 68-83.
[http://dx.doi.org/10.3991/ijet.v12i03.6434]

Izhar, T.A.T., Shoid, M.S.M. (2016). A Research Framework on Big Data awareness and Success Factors toward the Implication of Knowledge Management: Critical Review and Theoretical Extension. *Int. J. Acad. Res. Bus. Soc. Sci., 6*(4), 325-338.
[http://dx.doi.org/10.6007/IJARBSS/v6-i4/2111]

Kalaian, S.A., Kasim, R.M., Kasim, N.R. (2019). Descriptive and predictive analytical methods for big data. *In Web Services: Concepts, Methodologies, Tools, and Applications* IGI global.(pp. 314-331). USA:
[http://dx.doi.org/10.4018/978-1-5225-7501-6.ch018]

Moreno, A., Redondo, T. (2016). Text analytics: the convergence of big data and artificial intelligence. *International Journal of Interactive Multimedia and Artificial Intelligence, 3*(6), 57-64.
[http://dx.doi.org/10.9781/ijimai.2016.369]

Murumba, J., Micheni, E. (2017). Big Data Analytics in Higher Education: A Review. *Int. J. Eng. Sci. (Ghaziabad), 6*(6), 14-21. a
[http://dx.doi.org/10.9790/1813-0606021421]

Murumba, J., Micheni, E. (2017). Big Data Analytics in Higher Education: A Review. *Int. J. Eng. Sci. (Ghaziabad), 6*(6), 14-21. b
[http://dx.doi.org/10.9790/1813-0606021421]

Oi, M., Yamada, M., Okubo, F., Shimada, A., Ogata, H. (2017). Reproducibility of findings from educational big data. *proceedings of the Seventh International Learning Analytics & Knowledge Conference* (pp. 536-537). New York: ACM.
[http://dx.doi.org/10.1145/3027385.3029445]

O'Leary, D.E. (2013). Artificial intelligence and big data. *IEEE Intell. Syst., 28*(2), 96-99.
[http://dx.doi.org/10.1109/MIS.2013.39]

Rahman, N. (2016). Factors affecting Big Data technology adoption, 0-29. Available from:

http://pdxscholar.library.pdx.edu/studentsymposium%5Cnhttp://pdxscholar.library.pdx.edu/studentsymposium/2016/Presentations/10

Rani, B., Kant, S. (2020). An approach toward integration of big data into decision making process. *New Paradigm in Decision Science and Management.* (pp. 207-215). Singapore: Springer.
[http://dx.doi.org/10.1007/978-981-13-9330-3_19]

Sam, K.M., Chatwin, C.R. (2018). Understanding Adoption of Big Data Analytics in China: From Organizational Users Perspective. *IEEE International Conference on Industrial Engineering and Engineering Management,* Bangkok, Thailand507-510.
[http://dx.doi.org/10.1109/IEEM.2018.8607652]

Santos, A.F.C., Teles, Í.P., Siqueira, O.M.P., de Oliveira, A.A. (2018). Big data: A systematic review. *Advances in Intelligent Systems and Computing, 558*, 501-506.
[http://dx.doi.org/10.1007/978-3-319-54978-1_64]

Sun, S., Cegielski, C.G., Jia, L., Hall, D.J. (2018). Understanding the Factors Affecting the Organizational Adoption of Big Data. *J. Comput. Inf. Syst., 58*(3), 193-203.
[http://dx.doi.org/10.1080/08874417.2016.1222891]

Tornatzky, L.G., Fleischer, M. (1990). *The Processes of Technological Innovation.* (Vol. 3, pp. 27-50). Lexington: Lexington Books.

Verma, S., Bhattacharyya, S.S., Kumar, S. (2018). An extension of the technology acceptance model in the big data analytics system implementation environment. *Inf. Process. Manage., 54*(5), 791-806.
[http://dx.doi.org/10.1016/j.ipm.2018.01.004]

Vikas, G. (2021). Big Data Analytics in Education Market. Available from: https://www.alliedmarketresearch.com/big-data-analytics-in-education-market

Venkatesh, V., Bala, H. (2008). Technology acceptance model 3 and a research agenda on interventions. *Decis. Sci., 39*(2), 273-315.
[http://dx.doi.org/10.1111/j.1540-5915.2008.00192.x]

Venkatesh, V., Davis, F.D. (2000). A theoretical extension of the technology acceptance model: Four longitudinal field studies. *Manage. Sci., 46*(2), 186-204.
[http://dx.doi.org/10.1287/mnsc.46.2.186.11926]

Venkatesh, V., Morris, M.G., Davis, G.B., Davis, F.D. (2003). User acceptance of information technology: Toward a unified view. *Manage. Inf. Syst. Q., 27*(3), 425-478.
[http://dx.doi.org/10.2307/30036540]

Venkatesh, V., Thong, J.Y.L., Xu, X. (2012). Consumer acceptance and use of information technology: Extending the unified theory of acceptance and use of technology. *Manage. Inf. Syst. Q., 36*(1), 157-178.
[http://dx.doi.org/10.2307/41410412]

Verma, S., Bhattacharyya, S.S. (2017). Perceived strategic value-based adoption of Big Data Analytics in emerging economy. *J. Enterp. Inf. Manag., 30*(3), 354-382.
[http://dx.doi.org/10.1108/JEIM-10-2015-0099]

Verhoef, P.C., Kannan, P.K., Inman, J.J. (2015). From multi-channel retailing to omni-channel retailing: Introduction to the special issue on multi-channel retailing. *J. Retailing, 91*(2), 174-181.
[http://dx.doi.org/10.1016/j.jretai.2015.02.005]

Williamson, B. (2018). The hidden architecture of higher education: building a big data infrastructure for the 'smarter university'. *Int. J. Educ. Technol. High. Educ., 15*(1), 12.
[http://dx.doi.org/10.1186/s41239-018-0094-1]

Wamuyu, P.K., Maharaj, M. (2011). Factors influencing successful use of mobile technologies to facilitate E-Commerce in small enterprises: The case of Kenya. *African Journal of Information Systems, 3*, 48-71.

Wamba, S.F., Gunasekaran, A., Akter, S., Ren, S.J., Dubey, R., Childe, S.J. (2017). Big data analytics and firm performance: Effects of dynamic capabilities. *J. Bus. Res., 70*, 356-365.

[http://dx.doi.org/10.1016/j.jbusres.2016.08.009]

Wang, Y., Kung, L., Byrd, T.A. (2018). Big data analytics: Understanding its capabilities and potential benefits for healthcare organizations. *Technol. Forecast. Soc. Change, 126*, 3-13.
[http://dx.doi.org/10.1016/j.techfore.2015.12.019]

Xu, L.D., Duan, L. (2019). Big data for cyber physical systems in industry 4.0: a survey. *Enterprise Inf. Syst., 13*(2), 148-169.
[http://dx.doi.org/10.1080/17517575.2018.1442934]

Yang, F., Du, Y.R. (2016). Storytelling in the age of big data. *Asia Pacific Media Educator, 26*(2), 148-162.
[http://dx.doi.org/10.1177/1326365X16673168]

Yassine, A., Singh, S., Hossain, M.S., Muhammad, G. (2019). IoT big data analytics for smart homes with fog and cloud computing. *Future Gener. Comput. Syst., 91*(2), 563-573.
[http://dx.doi.org/10.1016/j.future.2018.08.040]

Yadegaridehkordi, E., Nilashi, M., Shuib, L., Hairul Nizam Bin Md Nasir, M., Asadi, S., Samad, S., Fatimah Awang, N. (2020). The impact of big data on firm performance in hotel industry. *Electron. Commerce Res. Appl., 40*, 100921.
[http://dx.doi.org/10.1016/j.elerap.2019.100921]

Zheng, M., Bender, D. (2019). Evaluating outcomes of computer-based classroom testing: Student acceptance and impact on learning and exam performance. *Med. Teach., 41*(1), 75-82.
[http://dx.doi.org/10.1080/0142159X.2018.1441984] [PMID: 29533105]

Zhang, M. (2015). Internet use that reproduces educational inequalities: Evidence from big data. *Comput. Educ., 86*(1), 212-223.
[http://dx.doi.org/10.1016/j.compedu.2015.08.007]

CHAPTER 7

The Adoption of the Internet of Things (IoT) in the Education Sector

Abstract: The Internet of Things (IoT) is causing a sea change in the educational system. IoTs are revolutionizing the classroom by making lessons more interactive and interesting for both teachers and students. An understanding of why IoT is becoming a vital component of daily instruction and learning is gained in this chapter, along with a discussion of the challenges and relevance of the technology in question. According to the study's findings, students can work together in real-time thanks to IoT devices. Smart whiteboards, for instance, enable collaborative brainstorming, note-taking, and writing amongst a group of people. Moreover, VR programs can imitate real-world circumstances, providing pupils with a more comprehensive education. Teachers can tailor their lessons to each student's individual needs with the aid of IoT devices. Teachers can make a greater impact on student's academic performance and engagement if they take into account how their students learn best. There are various ways in which humankind will profit from IoT development, but these gains will not be free. Some of the biggest drawbacks of the Internet of Things are security concerns, technological dependency, and employment insecurity. Governments throughout the world are investing time and energy to find solutions to these challenges and unlock the full potential of the IoTs. The capacity to employ Internet of Things technologies to create an interesting, dynamic learning environment is crucial for the future of education. Incorporating Internet of Things (IoT) devices into the classroom allows teachers to provide a more individualized, collaborative learning environment that boosts student engagement and achievement.

Keywords: Education, IoTs, Internet, Students, Teachers, Technology.

1. INTRODUCTION

The advent of digital tools has influenced new approaches to and goals for learning. Intelligent devices, IoT, Artificial Intelligence (AI), augmented reality (AR), virtual reality (VR), blockchain technology, and computer programs are just a few examples of the adaptable and disruptive advances in technology that have created new possibilities for enhancing education (Gaol & Prasolova-Frland, 2021; OECD, 2021). Therefore, in recent years, educational institutions around the world have made it a priority of their educational objectives to adopt approaches or regulations about technological integration (European Commission,

2019) and boost the amount they invest in ICT incorporation (Fernández-Gutiérrez *et al.*, 2020; Lawrence & Tar, 2018). Opportunities for HEIs to improve infrastructure robustness, scalability, and agility while maintaining autonomy are greatly enhanced by the Internet of Things (IoT). According to Villa-Henriksen *et al.* (2020), the IoT "enables both humans and objects to connect with virtually any place, at any moment, and any place; connectivity with everything and to anybody without a specific path and service." More than that, the Internet of Things broadens the reach of online education to more learners and more procedures (Al-Emran *et al.*, 2020). In addition to reducing expenses, the IoT allows students the flexibility to attend class from anywhere, including on campus, at home, or even on public transportation. Therefore, the Internet of Things is predicted to provide remedies that will transform pedagogical practices (Ramlowat & Pattanayak, 2019). The Internet of Things (IoT) is revolutionizing the educational experience for both students and teachers. Learning is made easier and more interesting through the technology's use of internet-connected physical gadgets and objects. The current significant increase in IoT use can be attributed to two factors: the constant pressure to innovate and the universal aspiration to improve one's degree of intelligence (Campbell, 2022). This chapter discusses the barriers and significance of IoT and gains insights into why this technology is becoming an integral part of daily learning and teaching methodologies.

2. LITERATURE

2.1. Internet of Things (IoT)

To link and share data across many different devices and systems over the internet, the "Internet of Things" (IoT) consists of a network of such devices and objects that contain software, sensors, and other technologies (Campbell, 2022). The term "smart home" might refer to appliances like smart fridges and voice-controlled assistants, or it can refer to more intricate industrial structures like robots and buyer-grade devices. The Internet of Things, or IoT, is a network of physical objects equipped with varying degrees of processing power, memory, communications capabilities, and other hardware and software components to exchange and assemble data. Financial services, tourism, education, telecommunications, and many more all make use of IoT in some way. The main argument for deploying IoT in the education sector is that it improves both the quality of education and the value of the physical facilities and the surrounding environment. When all systems are employed in a smart school (one that employs IoT), students are more likely to benefit from individualized instruction. Wi-Fi networks are utilized by the campus's smart gadgets to communicate with one another and receive commands (Ravindra, 2023) and data (Ravindra, 2022). Colleges and universities can benefit greatly from implementing an IoT computational nervous system because of the many ways in which it can aid in managing institutional resources, pedagogy, campus safety, and information dissemination. IoT, with its cutting-edge capabilities, might be seen as a different approach to managing a school.

2.2. Adoption of Internet of Things in the Education Sector

It is undeniable that the Internet has become the preferred method of interaction for scientists and engineers. The IoT is a dynamic force in the educational landscape. Traditional educational methods are becoming more effective and accessible as a result of the widespread adoption of internet-based technologies. Utilizing IoT in the classroom has been a revolutionary step forward. After the pandemic, several schools quickly adopted IoT solutions to improve safety and efficiency. To make life easier for administrators, educators, pupils, and parents, they implemented Internet of Things (IoT)-enabled gadgets into their educational infrastructure (Campbell, 2022). The Internet of Things (IoT) is now the spotlight attraction online. It will soon lay a solid groundwork for us all, and our lives will be completely revolutionized as a result. The Internet of Things is a powerful resource that can ease the burden of living in today's fast-paced world. It has the potential to create a fantastic situation, but it also has some drawbacks. Keep in mind that the Internet of Things is still a very novel concept that is only just beginning to get traction in terms of adoption. When it comes to incorporating Internet of Things (IoT) devices into their workflow, the education industry is among the most innovative and effective. This is because educators in this field recognize the potential for these tools to make learning more inclusive, collaborative, and engaging for students of all backgrounds. Using IoT devices, educators can track their student's progress in real time and ensure they have constant access to relevant content and effective means of communication. Based on IoT admission systems, flipped classes, orangery heating systems, and student feedback, this article examines innovative applications of IoT, the campus model, and the adoption of IoT at universities. Additionally, the results of both regular schooling and IoT flipped classrooms are evaluated based on student comments. Smart buildings, smart learning, sustainability, technological awareness, and waste and water management are only a few of the advantages of IoT applications that are addressed in the article (Zhamanov *et al.*, 2017). Lei *et al.* (2017) make a similar case for using flipped classes to better educate students about the Internet of Things. There are fourteen students registered in the IoT development course, and the instructors are making good use of the opportunity to tailor instruction to the diverse learning styles and needs of their students through group work, one-on-one discussions, and coaching. Finally, the IoTs development course contributes to better educational outcomes.

2.3. Benefits of IoTs in the Education Sector

• Facilitated Cooperation and Enhanced Dialogue

IoT gadgets like smart whiteboards, tablets, and laptops can improve communication and cooperation between instructors and students in real time. A smart whiteboard could be used by a teacher, for instance, to demonstrate concepts to students. Using their tablets, the students could participate in class discussions, exchange ideas, and work together on projects. This technology can facilitate communication between educators and their pupils and in group projects among students from different locations. Students from all over the world can work together in real time thanks to the elimination of physical distances (Nagar, 2023) due to this technology. Using the Internet of Things necessitates the use of the creation of mobile application services.

• Learning through Doing These days

however, there is much more to education than just a mashup of visuals and words. Several textbooks now have online companion sites that provide further learning resources like movies, materials, animations, tests, and more. For the students, this means more opportunities to learn about and discuss topics of interest with their peers and faculty. Teachers talk about issues students will face in everyday life and require them to research and present solutions. IoTs have the potential to greatly enhance the learning experience. It maintains pupils' interest in learning and, in the long run, aids in character development and cognitive acuity. Virtual classrooms are accessible from TVs and mobile devices, allowing for uninterrupted education even when a learner is ill. With IoT-based graphic classrooms, textbooks come to life with 3D pictures, colors, and noises, making learning more engaging. Voice-to-text processors and similar apps make it easier and faster to jot down notes.

• Boost Management Effectiveness

Keeping an educational institution running well is a laborious and paper-intensive procedure. There is a great deal of paperwork, inventory management, and budget allocation involved in running a school. IoTs solutions pave the way for a streamlined, risk-free, and collaborative decision-making framework in which all parties involved (instructors, students, parents, and government authorities) work together to enhance the condition of the building. Leaders will need to monitor the flow of money, keep tabs on inventory, keep detailed records of each student's attendance and performance in class, *etc.* (Campbell, 2022). By analyzing collected data and drawing conclusions to improve operations, educational institutions can use IoT to complete management duties more quickly and with less uncertainty. Students, parents, administrators, and faculty are all better informed as a result.

• Management of Disabilities

When creating instructional materials, it is common practice to overlook the needs of children with disorders like dyslexia. The Internet of Things allows the development of adapted applications to support the education of kids with special needs. Students with hearing impairments can read transcripts of lectures and lectures from other sources that have been converted to text. Blind students can benefit from a sound-to-voice converter. Apps tailored to the needs of impaired kids are revolutionizing the way they learn. Studying these apps can be helpful for education.

• Exam and Attendance Evaluation

Some schools require a certain percentage of students to pass each semester, have perfect attendance, *etc.* Internet of Things software collects and reports on student attendance. Students with low attendance rates are notified, and all students can monitor their progress *via* apps built with IoT technology. With the use of IoTs, students may now submit their exam answers from afar. Sensors embedded in various gadgets can monitor a student's whereabouts to detect any attempts at cheating.

• Obtaining Data in Real Time

IoT devices in the classroom allow for the precise collection and management of massive amounts of data. In addition, gigabytes of data can be processed concurrently by these devices (Campbell, 2022). Institutions can more easily monitor things like students' whereabouts and attendance, as well as teachers' effectiveness and the effectiveness of training programs. With this information, they can refine their teaching strategies and offer more effective professional development opportunities for teachers. With IoT's ability to handle terabytes of data concurrently, it is now possible to implement a wide range of safety and academic monitoring systems in universities and colleges. The efficiency of testing and grading may be increased, and new methods of classroom participation can be explored with the use of real-time data used by ministries and administrators. Most of the curricula and methods of instruction used in schools today are antiquated, which is a major problem. What this means is that the material is inappropriate for today's students. With the use of IoTs, data can be collected and analyzed to provide lessons that place a premium on student collaboration, strengthen concentration, and expand learning opportunities. The Internet of Things is also useful for gathering information about faculty and students to better produce school-related devices, accessories, and data by catering to their preferences.

• **Connectivity on a Global Scale**

Because of the Internet of Things' global reach, educators may standardize their practices to produce more effective education for students everywhere. Education professionals throughout the world can benefit from peer-to-peer training tools made possible by the IoTs. On the other hand, students will be able to exchange course materials across borders, making education more widely available.

• **Managing Our Resources Efficiently**

Money is a crucial component in the smooth operation of any educational institution. It has significant energy needs, as well as high storage and operation expenses (Campbell, 2022). The IoTs can be used to reduce the wasteful use of resources like energy and water in the academic sector. This is also an excellent move in the direction of protecting the natural world. Using IoT in the classroom helps schools run more smoothly and save money on utilities and space. Facility managers can also use IoT devices for occupant training to reduce wasteful water and power use.

• **Enhanced Availability**

These days, classrooms are not the only places where people can learn. Instead, people from all around the world can access the internet and learn at their own pace. IoTs are a system that links electronic gadgets and other physical objects to the web to help people get things done (Campbell, 2022). Due to the ubiquitous nature of IoT-enabled systems, teachers can reach more students and raise their professional standards. Teachers can network and share ideas to improve instruction. At the same time, students have greater flexibility and speedier course access (Campbell, 2022). In addition, they have the option of forming virtual study groups with other students.

• **Adaptive Instruction**

Teachers and school administrators can gain insight into each student's learning preferences, development, and trouble spots with the use of IoT devices. Using this data, educators may design engaging and effective instruction that meets the specific needs of each student. If a student is having trouble grasping a particular subject, teachers can tailor their instruction to meet that student's needs (Nagar, 2023) by providing them with supplementary materials and assistance. On the other side, if a student is showing exceptional proficiency in a given area, they may be given access to more advanced material. As a whole, tailored education can guarantee that every kid gets the attention and direction they need to flourish in school. Students are more likely to be invested and motivated if the content they are learning is directly applicable to their lives and interests.

- **Monitor Students' Activities**

Whether a student is accessing the online portal from inside or outside of the school's physical location, teachers are always able to keep tabs on what they are up to and how much time they are spending on any given subject. IoT sensors in the classroom gather information and make recommendations for pupils based on their interests and strengths (Muskan, 2021). It is also simple to figure out who participated in a certain evaluation, as well as keep score and monitor development. To limit kids' access to the internet for inappropriate or pointless purposes, schools are beginning to restrict internet access on student cellphones that are connected to campus Wi-Fi to apps designed for that reason. Devices can be customized with parental controls and instructor monitoring features to support only selected software and systems.

- **Increased Participation in the Classroom**

Teachers can keep their pupils interested and motivated with the help of IoT devices like interactive whiteboards and tablets (Nagar, 2023) by making their teachings more interesting and dynamic. A teacher could utilize an IWB to show students films or images to better explain a concept, for instance. Then, they can utilize their tablets or other electronic devices to answer questions, take part in class discussions, or finish off lesson-related interactive tasks. Students can work together on assignments and share materials and knowledge in real time with the help of e-learning systems that incorporate IoT technologies. It has the potential to improve classroom dynamics, making them more open and interesting places for learning and problem-solving. Using IoT technology in the classroom can improve learning results and student satisfaction (Nagar, 2023) by encouraging greater student participation.

- **Better Allocation of Available Resources**

Teachers and school administrators have better visibility and control over classroom supplies because of IoT technology. IoTs-based school management solutions, for instance, may monitor the circulation of books and other classroom resources and notify teachers when they are running low. By preventing pupils from having to duplicate resources, it helps save money and eliminate waste (Nagar, 2023) in the classroom. Classrooms, laboratories, and athletic facilities are just some of the places where IoT technologies can be put to use for monitoring and management. It can assist in maximizing the usefulness of these assets and make their utilization more efficient. Saving money and making better use of available resources are just two outcomes of better resource management made possible by using IoT systems in the education sector (Nagar, 2023) through the usage of IoT systems.

- **Improved Security and Safety**

Schools can employ IoT devices to keep children and staff safe by keeping an eye on the premises and the buses. IoT-enabled security cameras, for instance, may keep an eye on campus buildings and grounds and report any unusual or suspicious activities to the proper authorities (Nagar, 2023). Due to the large number of pupils in any one classroom, it might be difficult to keep track of their whereabouts and activities. Moreover, compared to the population at any other place of employment, students in an educational institution are more exposed to hazards and require smart security (Ravindra, 2023). IoTs have great potential to improve safety in educational institutions of all kinds. Similarly, IoT-enabled GPS tracking systems can keep tabs on school buses, protecting children as they ride to and from class. Using smart locks and other security systems, IoT technology can monitor and manage who has access to school premises. Therefore, it can aid in blocking off intruders and safeguarding against dangers. In summary, Nagar (2023) argues that schools will have the resources they need to keep their children and staff safe if they use IoT technologies. Technologies like 3D location allow for round-the-clock monitoring of students and instantaneous reporting of their whereabouts. In the event of an emergency, these systems can also include panic buttons (Ravindra, 2023) for quick response. Intelligent camera vision can be employed on campus to keep an eye on student conduct. Computer vision technology has come a long way recently and can now track any changes made to a signature. Any unforeseen occurrences can be prevented immediately by performing this action. Safety in schools is important not only for the people who work there but also for the building itself and the technology it uses. Attackers are smarter now therefore traditional methods are frequently insufficient (Campbell, 2022). Tracking devices, video monitoring tools, vaping sensors, surveillance cameras, and other smart systems made possible by the Internet of Things may help you keep tabs on everything at your school around the clock, ensuring the safety of your children, faculty, and physical space. As a result, everyone involved, from students to educators to parents, feel more secure in the school's environment.

• **Recording Attendance Mechanically**

Teaching is a full-time job in and of itself; therefore, keeping track of student attendance is a top priority for educators. IoTs can provide a means to simplify the laborious process of keeping track of attendance and calculating it for various uses. The IoTs can ease this burden for virtually every subject area. Students' attendance in class can be taken automatically using biometric attendance or barcodes based on their identification card numbers. This virtually eliminates storage and inconsistency issues (Muskan, 2021). Even though this will not free up teachers to focus on what they should be doing more—teaching students—direct communication between the school and their parents about their child's absence from class can improve the effectiveness of such systems. Teachers' attendance and class counts can be recorded using the same system, and so can the arrival and departure times of support workers at the school, all of which can be verified using biometrics.

• **Premises Safety**

Most educational institutions are not prepared for emergencies or disasters and lack the resources to spot warning signs of theft, abuse, sexual assault, and other crimes that might occur on campus. Because of a network system that allows the video recording to be presented at various displays in the premise, IoT can aid in solving such problems on a massive scale in the case of any unpleasant activity that gets observed on the camera. Alarms based on the IoTs can pinpoint the specific location of a fire or short circuit, making it easier and safer to put out the fire or repair the circuit. In addition, the smart door lock can be activated *via* sensors and alarms to automatically summon aid in the event of an attempted break-in at the school. This would provide not only peace of mind for those using the system but also a relief for the management structures that occasionally have to deal with such challenges.

• **Remote Instruction**

Institutions can provide their distance learners with access to IoT-based systems that store and format data in an application form with specialized software and in the form of a sign-in feature of websites (Muskan, 2021). Those who are unable to enroll in a traditional school but would still like to further their education can benefit from this. A well-rounded strategy for distance learners can include live and recorded lessons, online evaluation questions with timers, and monitoring of portal usage.

- **Keeping Tabs on the Well-Being of Faculty and Students**

A school with a healthy student body and teaching staff will be more effective in its mission. For students to be more engaged in class, they must take care of their health daily. Students' well-being is detected and tracked using physiological signs. Doctors can more easily analyze students' health with this data saved in databases. The Internet of Things can also be used to keep track of vital signs, medical history, allergies, and prescription information in case of an emergency.

- **Cost Savings in Operation**

To maximize profits, educational institutions can benefit from the development of IoT technology by lowering operational and other costs. Every school strives to save costs wherever possible, but only those that make extensive use of IoT solutions do so successfully (Pedamkar, 2023). To lower the school's operational costs, constant connectivity to the smart device and organization is required.

- **Increased Safety Precautions**

The Internet of Things makes it possible for the access control system to boost safety measures at the university and for the general public. Using IoT technology in surveillance can boost internal security and make it easier to monitor any unusual behavior. An employee's daily activities can be recorded and monitored, which is helpful in an academic setting. Furthermore, it can be managed remotely thanks to internet connectivity. The goal of preserving the company's security can be realized in this way (Pedamkar, 2023). The IoTs can improve security measures and reduce the possibility of security breaches in schools (Pedamkar, 2023) if used properly. In the construction industry, for example, sensors and wearable technology can be utilized to keep workers safe from harm. The security threshold can be raised by employing several cutting-edge Internet of Things solutions, and autonomous devices are required. The devices need to assess the situation and act accordingly. IoTs can act as a protective barrier between the general public and vulnerable institutions like schools.

- **Compiled Information**

Data is often referred to as the ultimate tool for any educational institution. When it comes to collecting information about their pupils and the services and materials they use in the classroom, educational institutions are big users of IoT models and approaches (Pedamkar, 2023). To extend their operations and increase their profits, educational institutions collect and analyze a variety of data to better understand their customers and provide better services. The Internet of Things has unleashed a floodgate of prospects for brand-new markets and streams of income.

Revenue, profit, return on investments, and overall earnings for educational institutions can all be improved with the use of IoT-driven models.

• Focus on Student/Customer

An ever-present priority for any school should be the happiness of its students. Using cutting-edge IoT technologies, such as mobile card readers or smart trackers, to better serve customers. Using portable card readers, financial transactions performed *via* mobile devices can proceed quickly and easily. The intelligent tracker may be used to keep tabs on stock levels. The IoTs are being used by many universities to boost their future businesses and elevate the quality of their consumer experiences (Pedamkar, 2023). There are a variety of IoT solutions designed specifically for finding and fixing consumer problems. By connecting and coordinating these devices, IoT helps businesses streamline their operations. With the use of IoT devices, schools may collect feedback from kids to enhance their services and boost customer satisfaction. Weaknesses in the product can be readily identified and addressed.

• Increased Efficiency, Greater Productivity, and Better Communication

Many time-consuming administrative duties, such as tracking attendance and grading, can be automated by using IoT systems by instructors and administrators. It can let teachers devote more time to student instruction and other important responsibilities (Muskan, 2021). Using IoT system to automate attendance monitoring, for instance, frees teachers from having to manually take a roll each day. Similar to how using an IoT system to grade homework and tests expedites the process of providing feedback to students. Other administrative duties, like scheduling and communication, can be automated with the help of IoT technologies. It can help make the educational system more effective by decreasing the amount of time and effort spent on repetitive tasks (Muskan, 2021). As a whole, implementing IoT technologies in the educational sector can boost productivity, letting teachers devote more time to actual instruction and resulting in a better educational experience for pupils. Virtual classes delivered *via* apps on students' smartphones encourage more participation. When students have a deeper and more nuanced understanding of the material, they are better equipped to convey their thoughts and questions outside of the classroom. Scanning the codes on the books to access the digital version of the same can make students more interested in participating in exams, activities, and even self-learning. They have access to the materials provided by the teacher and can review the content whenever it is most convenient for them through the teacher's web portal. Students' productivity and skill development can both benefit from this approach.

3. DISADVANTAGES OF IOTS IN EDUCATION

While the Internet of Things has many benefits, it also has many downsides. The following are a few drawbacks of the IoT:

• Privacy Concerns

Connected devices in an IoT system exchange data with one another across a network. As a result, data sent between devices on the network is largely unprotected. Hackers now have more options than ever to enter into a network and steal sensitive information because of the proliferation of internet-connected devices (Pedamkar, 2023) due to the convergence of technology and social media. It is not always simple to keep linked with friends and relatives and provide them with every part of our life operation, especially if we want some personal space in life. Your information could very well end up in the wrong hands. Cybersecurity groups have put in place several safeguards and standards to limit the chances of sensitive information falling into the wrong hands. However, hackers will always be able to find a way to exploit a flaw in the system. For instance, the hacking collective known as "Anonymous" breached government databases and released sensitive material. The government's top security plan did not prevent the breach, and the security framework was compromised (Pedamkar, 2023) despite the government's best efforts. Therefore, if everything is kept online, hackers may quickly break in and learn everything about everyone's lives. Companies may attempt to take advantage of people by misusing the information they have access to. This is an increasingly common blunder in workplaces nowadays. Google, for instance, has recently been under fire for allegedly exploiting customers' personal information.

• The Rising Cost of Technology

Regarding schooling, times have changed considerably. Pens, paper, and books were formerly all that was needed to educate a student. However, with the advent of technology in the classroom, there are now many additional tools that students must have. Every college student nowadays should have a laptop or computer because digital education is quickly replacing the paper-based model. It is not cheap for students to buy and maintain their electronic devices, let alone pay for the software needed to use them. Tuition expenses are necessary to cover the costs of providing students with increasingly sophisticated technical resources. Instead, a student's resources would be better served by investing in other areas.

• Over-Dependence on Technology

The current generation has everything they need at their disposal. One may quickly and easily access data and media anywhere, be it Google results or a past episode of "Game of Thrones". The ready-to-use calculators on our devices make quick work of basic arithmetic operations like adding and subtracting. People are becoming overly reliant on technology, thanks to developments in the Internet of Things, to do even the most basic of jobs, such as turning off the lights or driving a car. Only a few academics have predicted that the Internet of Things will eventually make people lazy and unmotivated to work. However, making decisions based on the data provided by technology daily might have devastating consequences. There is no foolproof system available. The internet, in particular, seems to be particularly prone to technical breakdowns. The more dependent we are on the Internet, the worse the consequences could be if it were to suddenly disappear. As more and more devices get connected to the internet, everyone's private information will be accessible from anywhere in the world. It is possible to monitor every move of a user in their own home (Pedamkar, 2023) with relative ease. IoT gadgets and their backers (companies) are aware of your every waking and sleeping moment, as well as every step you take indoors and outside.

• Unemployment

In many sectors, IoT robots have largely supplanted human labor. This results in factory worker layoffs and, in some cases, lower wages for similarly skilled workers. As more and more things become connected and the internet, fewer people will be needed to operate them, and some employment may be lost as a result. With the rise of IoT and AI, all tasks currently performed by humans will be automated. Chatbots are already doing a lot of the work in occupations previously occupied by humans, like customer service (Pedamkar, 2023). Workers with low to moderate levels of education will be hit particularly hard by automation. Devices will not only be able to communicate with each other but will also update inventory information to the owner at regular intervals, perhaps putting the jobs of individuals who work in warehouses as inventory evaluators in jeopardy. Robotic machines, which function automatically in the grocery checkout line and even at ATMs, are a major contributor to the current employment downturn. Current and future IoT technologies are predicted to significantly alter practically every facet of how universities function. High unemployment rates are a result of the high vulnerability of all workers, regardless of their level of education or training. Humans are being supplanted by technological innovations, such as smart surveillance cameras, robotics, ironing systems, washing machines, and more.

• **Inadequate Methods of Instruction**

In the past, teachers had nothing but facts at their disposal to impart to their students. It was an effective method. However, some of these educators will need to acquire the necessary technological expertise, which can take some time. Educators struggle to incorporate mechanization into their lessons. Students, on the other hand, are adept at using technology but struggle to learn from it.

• **False or Misleading Data**

Today's websites care more about their search engine rankings than they do about the content they provide. To attract more visitors, some websites are publishing false or inaccurate data online (Walter, 2020). As a student, you may visit websites that present inaccurate or misleading data. Some websites steal the work of others without verifying the accuracy of the materials. The misinformation is harmful to students either way.

• **Additional Distractions for the Classroom**

The proliferation of internet-connected gadgets is largely attributable to technological advancements. Most of the time, students have trouble maintaining concentration. Students, just like a writer at write-my-paper-for-me.com, have to block out background noise and other interruptions to get their work done. Computers and mobile phones make things worse (Walter, 2020).

• **Students' Ineffective Approaches to Learning**

With just a few mouse clicks, students can access any resource, wherever in the world. They can now enjoy it without exerting any effort. Furthermore, students do not need to attend lectures as often because they may go online and receive information from many sources (Walter, 2020).

• **The Failure of Technology**

Many new inventions, especially technological ones, have bugs. For instance, many servers have issues and go down, which makes it difficult to study. Issues with establishing a connection are also common (Walter 2020). These problems will not go away overnight. This causes a delay in education. Companies can help new hires with hybrid and remote work overcome communication barriers by using training video software.

• **Facilitates Cheating**

When students were unable to use their phones to access the internet during exams, cheating was far more difficult. Students are using the latest technologies to "game" the system. Detecting and proving student dishonesty has grown increasingly difficult (Walter, 2020). As a result, many dishonest students graduate with degrees. They eventually become full-fledged experts in the fields despite being intellectually unqualified for them.

• **The Disparity in National Norms**

Due to the lack of a universally accepted compatibility standard for the Internet of Things, interoperability issues arise when trying to link products from different manufacturers.

• **Decreased Capacity for Thought and Action**

People become lazy and unmotivated when they rely too heavily on their smartphones and other electronic devices instead of engaging in constructive activities.

• **Security Breach**

In the IoT, real-world items are linked to the web so they may exchange data. Because of this, hackers now have access to the user database, which contains very sensitive data. When unauthorized parties gain access to sensitive user information, this is known as a data breach. The user can be influenced by this information.

• **Dependence**

Connectivity to the internet is crucial for the IoT to function. IoT gadgets cannot do their jobs without a reliable internet connection.

• **Complexity**

Even though IoT devices appear to be performing complex activities, a massive collection of complex processes occurs in the background to make this possible. Users often need to contact customer support even for relatively simple issues since they are unaware of the underlying mechanism. If the program makes a mistake in its calculation, the entire object will stop working. As a result, it is difficult because of all the code and the interoperability issues between the numerous devices. If a single node in a network goes down, it affects the whole system. Due to the IoT system's inherent complexity, it is not easy to design, build, manage, and enable a comprehensive IoT system.

• **Inadequate Global Norms**

There is currently no universal set of IoT standards to ensure interoperability. As a result, producers in diverse fields have trouble communicating with one another.

• **Decreased Capacity for Thought and Action**

Internet and IoT addiction has led to a sedentary lifestyle. The reduction in physical activity caused by the increased use of IoT has serious consequences for people's health. Stress levels in humans may rise as a result of this for several reasons.

4. IMPLICATIONS

Smart expansion is now possible in every industry thanks to cutting-edge technological developments. Along with other industries, education is flourishing thanks to recent innovations. As a result, the personal nature of technology has resulted in several shifts across industries. The Edtech industry's necessity for and importance to the education area became increasingly apparent over time. IoT is a rapidly evolving field wherein digital resources are being used in classrooms. Additionally, it provides a more powerful boost to the conventional schooling system. In today's modern world, online courses have replaced traditional classroom instruction. This includes a combination of real-time instruction, lecture recordings, virtual problem solutions, *etc.*, all accessible *via* a shared server and dedicated desktop applications. As a result, the landscape of education is shifting rapidly. The Internet of Things is allowing education to become more practically applicable and, in certain circumstances, to go outside the confines of traditional educational institutions, both of which have benefited much from technological advancements. IoTs have emerged as a vital tool for meeting the requirements of academic institutions and their students. As a result, the standard of education in underdeveloped regions benefits. The educational system was maintained because of IoT, even when coronavirus dominated the world. With the help of IoT, students may study from the comfort of their own homes, and the Internet has made available a wealth of resources to aid in their education. The Ministry of Higher Education and university administrators could benefit from a better understanding of the elements that affect IoT as they formulate policy. Also, learning analytics driven by the IoTs can help spot problems before they become too much for a student to handle. Using this information, teachers may determine which students are having difficulty in class and give them the help they need to catch up or better grasp the material at hand. IoT-enabled learning analytics can also be used to tailor instruction to each learner. Teachers can better satisfy their students' individual needs if they have a thorough awareness of each pupil's aptitudes, areas of struggle, and areas of interest.

CONCLUSION

This chapter explains why the IoTs are so important and how they may be used to improve education by creating smarter, more interactive, and more conducive learning institutions. With the help of the IoT, today's schools can evolve into smarter, more efficient learning institutions of the future.

Integrating intelligent systems for lighting, heating, air conditioning, air quality monitoring, access control, *etc.*, with intelligent systems dealing with the learning process itself entails monitoring students' presence and behavior, noise and fidgeting in the classroom, students' interactions with the educational system, learning resources, *etc.*

All environmental factors and sensor data are monitored and controlled by a central server located in the cloud, which is also responsible for processing and interpreting the data. Keeping these considerations in mind, we introduced two prototype microcontroller devices and briefly outlined their capabilities and role in an IoT network.

Fear and anticipation, or both, are constant companions to any new development or trend, anticipating positive outcomes despite the potential dangers. The advent of the IoTs represents a sea change in the cutting-edge technological world. IoTs solutions for education have provided answers to improve education quality on a global scale by making it more accessible and simpler to comprehend.

Since the IoTs are a costly investment, some schools are adopting technology at their own speed. Due to the benefits and wide scope of IoTs, this is an area where investment is warranted. Because IoT-enabled gadgets can now provide teachers and students with advanced educational capabilities in environments that are both user-friendly and secure, a plethora of new educational platforms have emerged in recent years.

The IoT is reshaping how schools function and how teachers and students communicate. Better data gathering and analysis, increased automation of procedures, and communication between teachers, students, and administrators are all made possible by the IoT's ability to connect physical devices to the Internet. While the positive effects of the IoTs on classroom instruction cannot be denied, the technology is not without its downsides.

The ability to gather and analyze educational data is the primary benefit of the IoT in educational institutions. Connecting sensors and cameras allows schools to collect more detailed information about their student's progress and the efficiency of their teaching techniques. This information can be utilized to pinpoint problem areas and fine-tune teaching methods. Increased process automation is another benefit of the IoTs. Sensors and cameras, for instance, can be utilized to track student attendance and notify teachers and principals of any unexcused absences.

Classroom management and resource allocation are two other areas where automation can be put to use. As a result, both teachers and principals will have an easier time maintaining order in the classroom. Furthermore, the IoT facilitates enhanced interaction among educators, students, and administration. Teachers and students can work together and share resources more effectively through the use of linked devices because of the increased frequency and ease of communication between them. There are, however, certain possible negatives to think about when introducing the IoT into classrooms. For instance, students' personal information may become a privacy concern as a result of the widespread adoption of technological tools. In addition, many educational institutions may not be able to afford to adopt the IoT.

While the benefits of the IoT to schools are apparent, precautions must be taken to preserve students' privacy and keep expenditures to a minimum. IoT has the potential to dramatically improve teaching and learning if implemented correctly in schools.

REFERENCES

Al-Emran, M., Malik, S.I., Al-Kabi, M.N. (2020). *"A survey of Internet of Things (IoT) in education: Opportunities and challenges,"* in Toward Social Internet of Things (SIoT): Enabling Technologies, Architectures and Applications. (pp. 197-209). Cham: Springer. [http://dx.doi.org/10.1007/978-3-030-24513-9_12]

Campbell, A. (2022). Role and Impact of IoT in Education Industry. Available from: https://www.helpwire.app/blog/iot-in-education/

Lei, C-U., Yau, C-W., Lui, K-S., Yum, P., Tam, V., Yuen, A.H-K. (2017). Teaching internet of things: enhancing learning efficiency *via* full-semester flipped classroom *IEEE 6th International Conference on Teaching, Assessment, and Learning for Engineering (TALE),* Hong Kong, China56-60. [http://dx.doi.org/10.1109/TALE.2017.8252304]

Muskan. (2021). Applications of IoT in Education. Available from: https://www.analyticssteps.com/blogs/8-applications-iot-education

Nagar, T. (2023). Top 6 Things You Should Know About IoT In The Education Industry. Available from: https://elearningindustry.com/top-things-you-should-know-about-iot-in-the-education-industry

Pedamkar, P. (2023). IoT Disadvantages. Available from: https://www.educba.com/iot-disadvantages/

Ravindra, S. (2023). Role of IoT in Education. Available from: https://www.kdnuggets.com/2018/04/role-io--education.html

Ramlowat, D.D., Pattanayak, B.K. (2019). *"Exploring the internet of things (IoT) in education: a review,"* in *Information Systems Design and Intelligent Applications.* (pp. 245-255). Mauritius: Springer.
[http://dx.doi.org/10.1007/978-981-13-3338-5_23]

Villa-Henriksen, A., Edwards, G.T.C., Pesonen, L.A., Green, O., Sørensen, C.A.G. (2020). Internet of Things in arable farming: Implementation, applications, challenges and potential. *Biosyst. Eng., 191*, 60-84.
[http://dx.doi.org/10.1016/j.biosystemseng.2019.12.013]

Zhamanov, A., Sakhiyeva, Z., Suliyev, R., Kaldykulova, Z. (2017). IoT smart campus review and implementation of IoT applications into education process of university *13th International Conference on Electronics, Computer and Computation (ICECCO),* Abuja, Nigeria 1-4.
[http://dx.doi.org/10.1109/ICECCO.2017.8333334]

Walter, J. (2020). Disadvantages of Technology in Education. Available from: https://www.dejaoffice.com/blog/2020/10/28/7-disadvantages-of-technology-in-education/

SUBJECT INDEX

A

Abouzeid, business analysts 96
Acceptance, technological 100
Adaptive instruction 118
Adopting digital technologies 8
Adoption 55, 65, 70, 115
   difficulties 55
   of e-learning and e-teaching development 65
   of Internet of Things 115
   rate 70
AI-assisted 24, 77
   evaluation 77
   planners 24
AI-based 80, 82
   educational systems 80
   testing 82
AI-enhanced games 81
AI-powered 26, 78
   tutoring applications 26
   virtual personal assistants 78
Aid 19, 76, 106
   businesses 19, 106
   educators 76
Air conditioning 129
Analysis 4, 90
   bibliometric 4
   techniques 90
Appliances, electronic 61
Apps 21, 22, 32, 67, 70, 82, 99, 116, 117, 119, 123
   and platforms for learning and administration 32
   computer-related 70
   eLearning 22
   location-based 99
   mobile learning 21
Artificial intelligence 75, 77, 82
   features 75
   research 77
   software systems 82
   teaching system (AITS) 77
Attention deficit hyperactivity disorder (ADHD) 25
Augmented reality (AR) 3, 4, 6, 20, 23, 113
Automated speech recognition (ASR) 84
Automatic voice recognition 84

B

Big data 87, 88, 89, 91, 94, 95, 96, 98, 99, 100, 101, 102, 104, 105, 106, 108
   adopting 87
   analytics 88, 89, 91, 104, 105
   applications 100
   arena 101
   implementation 101
   initiatives 101
   procedure 108
   services 108
   technologies 88, 94, 95, 99, 102, 104, 106
   tools 94, 96, 98, 100, 101, 102
Business(s) 8, 9, 32, 34, 42, 46, 47, 48, 49, 54, 63, 91, 92, 99, 100, 101, 107, 123
   intelligence 46, 54, 91
   streamline 123

C

Chatbots and online tutors 78
Classroom 2, 3, 4, 5, 7, 10, 12, 13, 16, 17, 19, 20, 21, 25, 27, 40, 43, 46, 49, 50, 52, 55, 64, 76, 79, 80, 83, 84, 103, 115, 119, 130
   conditions 103
   devices 5
   dynamic 27
   dynamics 119
   efficiency 20, 46, 55
   flipped 115
   innovation 43
   instruction, virtual 7
   instructors 79

management and resource allocation 130
   physical 49
   settings, traditional 10, 49, 64
   traditional 21
Climate change 16
Cloud 2, 6, 71
   computing 2, 6
   hosting 71
Cognitive process 61
Collaborative 6, 79, 113
   brainstorming 113
   education 79
   learning activities 6
Combined TAM 97
   and the theory of planned behavior (CTAMTPB) 97
Commerce 55, 90, 100
  electronic 90
  mobile 100
Commercial transactions 95
Commodity, scarce 2
Common misconception 7
Communication 7, 10, 16, 17, 18, 21, 40, 46, 49, 50, 52, 54, 55, 59, 60, 61, 62, 64, 66, 67, 70, 76, 115, 116, 129, 130
  asynchronous 21, 62
  networks 67
  skills 18
  technology 40, 46, 50, 52, 55, 59, 60, 61, 64, 66, 67, 70, 76
Competence 12, 32, 40, 50, 52, 70, 96
  crucial 96
  digital 12, 40
Computer 17, 53, 71, 77, 85, 113
  based learning 85
  networks 53
  programs 113
  screen 17
  skills 71
  software 77
Computerized intelligence system 77
Conduct, reliability technology engineers 95
Context 11, 12, 18, 29, 32, 50, 60, 63, 64, 66, 68, 95, 100
  environmental 66, 100
  institutional 68
COVID-19 1, 12, 33, 38, 46
  effects 1
  pandemic 1, 33, 38, 46
Customers 8, 48, 100, 122, 123, 124
  exploiting 124
  wireless 100
Customized 3, 7
  instruction 3
  learning 7
Cutting-edge 27, 30, 43, 128
  digital products 43
  equipment 30
  technological developments 128
  web-based hubs 27
Cyberbullying 38

D

Data 8, 9, 101, 107
  management 101, 107
  mining 8, 107
  resources 9
Data processing 90, 94
  big 94
Data processing 94, 104
  applications 94
  tools 104
Data storage 95, 98, 101
  systems, traditional 98, 101
Data warehouse 98, 102
  architecture 102
  operation 98
Database systems, traditional 96
Design, effective learning 83
Devices 5, 31, 36, 37, 38, 39, 47, 113, 114, 115, 116, 117, 119, 122, 123, 124, 125, 127, 129
  autonomous 122
  electronic 31, 119, 124, 127
  mobile 5, 47, 116, 123
  prototype microcontroller 129
Diffusion of innovations (DOI) 93
Digital 1, 2, 3, 6, 8, 10, 11, 12, 18, 19, 23, 24, 29, 30, 34, 35, 36, 37, 38, 41, 42, 43, 46, 47, 48, 49, 53, 55, 77, 128
  businesses 36
  communication 18
  distant learning 41
  drift 42
  educational businesses 36
  maturity 34
  remote learning 37
  resources 23, 30, 36, 43, 53, 77, 128
  revolution 1, 2, 3, 10, 30, 46, 55

signage 6
technologies 2, 3, 10, 11, 12, 19, 29, 42, 43, 47, 48, 49, 55
transitions 1, 8, 11, 12, 30, 35
world 24, 38
Digital education 13, 25, 31, 34, 35, 37, 38, 39, 43, 50, 124
   ecosystem 50
Digital tools 2, 8, 10, 11, 12, 20, 24, 32, 46, 47, 82, 113
   cutting-edge 8
Digital transformation 12, 34, 53
   calls 34
   culture 12
   process 12, 53
Digitally-enhanced teaching 11
Digitization process 30
Distance learning 11, 17, 19, 38, 39, 60, 61, 78
   places 60
   programs 19
Dresner advisory services 90

E

Economy, digital 49
Educated forecasts 36
Education 1, 11, 12, 19, 23, 27, 34, 75, 115
   children's 27
   industry 12, 75, 115
   policy 11
   system 1, 23, 34
   technology 19
Educational 3, 4, 5, 17, 23, 30, 33, 35, 37, 40, 43, 48, 76, 83, 89, 91, 103, 104, 123
   big data (EBD) 4, 91
   initiatives 43
   methods 40
   procedures 104
   programs 23, 37, 43, 103
   resources 5, 17, 33, 35
   sector 3, 30, 48, 76, 83, 89, 123
Educational opportunities 4, 33, 79
   engaging 4
Educational system 12, 13, 23, 28, 32, 34, 42, 43, 47, 48, 49, 55, 61, 78, 88, 128, 129
   innovative preemptive 78
   sustainable 23
   traditional 55
   web-based 61

Educational technology 5, 7, 19, 21, 22, 27, 35, 36, 51
   landscape 36
Electronic 6, 7, 61
   badges 6
   learning 61
   newsletters 7
Elements 68, 89, 102
   educational context 89
   management-supported 68
   technology adoption taxonomy 102
Engagement, social 43
ENQA's definition 11
Enterprises, private sector 50
Entrepreneurial environment 100
Environmental 25
   degradation 25
   preservation 25
Environments 25, 43, 61, 65, 69, 79, 80, 92, 129
   electronic 61
   hyper-connected 43
Ethical learning systems 75
Expense, supply chain 101

F

Factors 11, 12, 33, 46, 47, 49, 50, 51, 59, 62, 63, 65, 66, 68, 69, 70, 87, 93, 100, 108, 129
   environmental 66, 100, 129
   ethical 108
   institutional 51
   social 93
   technical 33, 65
Fast-paced world 115
Fault tolerance 96
Features 7, 36, 89
   facial 89
   labor-intensive 36
   live chat 7
Feedback 21, 22, 27, 41, 83, 90, 92, 123
   audio-recorded 27
   constructive 90
   refinement process 41
Financial 33, 123
   management procedures 33
   transactions 123
Fixing consumer problems 123
Foolproof system 125

Framework 16, 116
  collaborative decision-making 116
  modern educational 16

G

Government policy decisions 50
Growth, socioeconomic 32

H

Hadoop distributed file system (HDFS) 98
Higher education institutions (HEIs) 1, 47, 49, 51, 87, 108, 114

I

ICT 10, 40, 46, 47, 50, 51, 52, 54, 55, 56, 59, 60, 61, 66, 67, 70, 71
  adopting 55
  adoption 47, 56
  based digital learning choices 46, 55
  in teaching and learning processes 52
  in teaching practice 52
  integration of 10, 40, 55
Individual's propensity 97
Industries, construction 122
Infinite resources 23
Influence, social 47, 68, 97, 102, 103
Influenced Italian teachers 52
Information 3, 32, 41, 42, 46, 49, 55, 59, 61, 62, 66, 69, 71, 87, 97
  communication 46
    digital 55
    resources 41, 71
  technologies 3, 32, 41, 42, 49, 61, 62, 97
  technology infrastructure 59, 66, 69
  technology resources 87
Infrastructure 1, 6, 33, 34, 36, 49, 53, 61, 63, 66, 67, 68, 96, 102, 108, 115
  cloud 36
  digital 6, 53
  educational 115
  technical 102
  technological 96
Innovation diffusion theory (IDT) 97
IoT 115, 119, 123, 128, 130
  addiction 128
  admission systems 115
  in educational institutions 130
  sensors 119
  technologies, implementing 123
IoT-based 116, 121
  graphic classrooms 116
  systems 121
IoT devices 68, 113, 115, 117, 118, 120, 123, 127
  for occupant training 118
IoT-enabled 118, 120, 128
  GPS tracking systems 120
  learning 128
  security cameras 120
  systems 118

L

e-learning 41, 52, 61, 62, 63, 64, 65, 66, 67, 68, 69, 70, 71, 96, 119
  adopting 62, 68
  curriculum 61
  environments 62, 64, 96
  infrastructure 71
  instructions 41
  policy 69
  resources 64
  systems 61, 62, 63, 65, 66, 67, 69, 70, 119
  technologies 62, 64
  tools 52
Learning environments 10, 12, 27, 41, 43, 51
  flexible 43
Learning management systems (LMSs) 7, 25, 27, 49, 64, 71

M

Machine learning 19, 49, 84, 85
Massive open online courses (MOOCs) 11, 61, 64

N

Natural language processing (NLP) 77, 78, 81, 84
  algorithms 81
Non-governmental organizations (NGOs) 50, 66

O

Online databases 17
Online education 75, 92
    activities 92
    system 75
Open educational resources (OER) 11, 39

P

Political commentary 44
Power 9, 24, 34, 66, 75, 81
    computational 81
    transformative 75
Problems, growing 38
Professional development 47
Psychological principles 91

R

Remote Instruction 121
Resource allocation 11, 130
Robot educator 3
Robotic machines 125

S

Sensor(s) 95, 114, 117, 120, 121, 122, 129, 130
    data 129
    vaping 120
Social cognitive theory (SCT) 97
Software 1, 95
    developers 95
    technologies 1

T

TAM, blends 60
Teachers stress 52
Technological 6, 95
    factors 95
    solutions 6

Technology 4, 5, 16, 99, 104, 113, 120, 122
    big data system 104
    blockchain 113
    computer vision 120
    electronic 16
    mobile 5, 99
    virtual reality 4
    wearable 122
Telecommunications 23, 41, 90, 114
Tools 78, 93, 120
    anti-plagiarism 78
    big data analytics 93
    video monitoring 120
Tracking technology 22
Traditional 1, 3, 42, 91, 115, 120
    educational methods 115
    methods 1, 3, 42, 91, 120
Transformation efforts 37
Transformative technologies 4

V

Video 6, 24, 36, 121
    conferencing programs 6
    games 24
    learning 24
    recording 121
    streaming 36
Virtual 7, 27, 79
    assistant 79
    learning environments (VLEs) 7, 27
Visualization-based learning 85

W

Web-based learning management systems 7
Wi-Fi networks 114
Wired internet-based information systems 100
Wireless transaction 100

www.ingramcontent.com/pod-product-compliance
Lightning Source LLC
Chambersburg PA
CBHW041123300426
44113CB00002B/38